NEW BRITAIN

PICTORIAL RESEARCH BY
ARLENE C. PALMER

"PARTNERS IN PROGRESS" BY
WILLIAM R. NEAGUS

PRODUCED IN COOPERATION WITH
FAMILY SERVICE, INC.

WINDSOR PUBLICATIONS, INC.
CHATSWORTH, CALIFORNIA

NEW BRITAIN

THE CITY OF INVENTION

An Illustrated History

by Patrick Thibodeau

To My Parents

Windsor Publications, Inc.—History Books Division
Managing Editor: Karen Story
Design Director: Alexander D'Anca
Photo Director: Susan L. Wells
Executive Editor: Pamela Schroeder

Staff for *New Britain: The City of Invention:*
Manuscript Editor: Douglas P. Lathrop
Photo Editor: Loren Prostano
Proofreader: Liz Reuben
Senior Editor, Corporate Biographies: Judith L. Hunter
Production Editor, Corporate Biographies: Albert J. Polito
Customer Service Manager: Phyllis Feldman-Schroeder
Editorial Assistants: Kim Kievman, Michael Nugwynne, Kathy B.
    Peyser, Susan Schlanger, Theresa J. Solis
Publisher's Representatives, Corporate Biographies: Bill Joeks,
    Bob Sadoski
Layout Artist, Corporate Biographies: Bonnie Felt
Layout Artist, Editorial: Michael Burg
Designer: Ellen Ifrah

Library of Congress Cataloging-in-Publication Data
Thibodeau, Patrick, 1954-
    New Britain : the city of invention : an illustrated history / by
    Patrick Thibodeau. —1st ed.
    p. 128   cm. 22 x 28
    Bibliography: p. 125
    Includes index.
    ISBN 0-89781-316-2
    1. New Britain (Conn.)—History. 2. New Britain (Conn.)—
Description—Views. 3. New Britain (Conn.)—Industries. I. Title.
F104.N5T48 1989   974.6′2—dc20   CIP
                                                   89-33702

Windsor Publications, Inc.
Elliot Martin, Chairman of the Board
James L. Fish III, Chief Operating Officer
Michele Sylvestro, Vice President/Sales-Marketing

*FRONTISPIECE: Located in the middle of downtown,
Central Park has always been an identifying landmark in
New Britain. Courtesy, Local History Room of the
New Britain Public Library*

*RIGHT: By 1899 New Britain was a booming industrial
city. This view of Main Street, looking south, illustrates
bustling turn-of-the-century activity. Courtesy, Local History
Room of the New Britain Public Library*

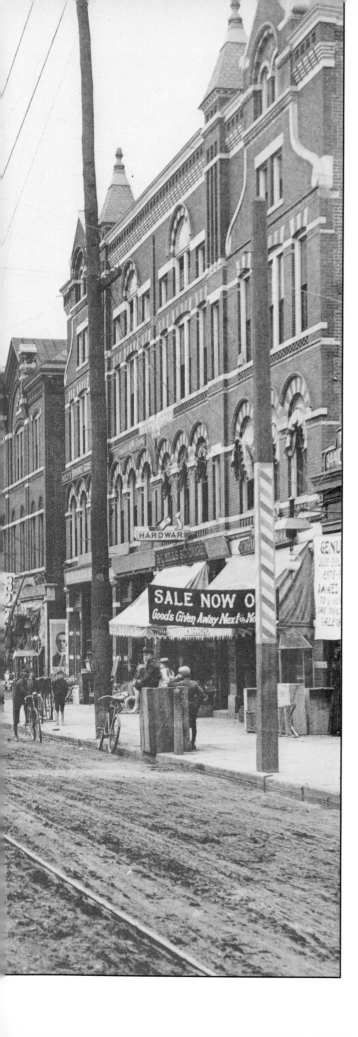

CONTENTS

PREFACE

New Britain was no one's first choice. Unlike Hartford, it had no major river. It lacked, as opposed to Farmington, any waterway large enough to drive a mill. Hills and rock outcrops were prevalent. Its early population growth was the result of expansions from more fertile farming areas. As time went on, the major roads through the area bypassed New Britain.

These limited natural advantages and the village's relative isolation may have prompted the men and women of early New Britain to be a little more resourceful and inventive. They were characteristics that future generations, and arriving immigrant groups, would inherit and make their own. Inventiveness, and all the components of it, have been a persistent trait of this city; without it there would have been no "Hardware City."

This book attempts to offer new insights and facts about the city's history. Many sections use material that has not appeared elsewhere. Perhaps most significant is a section in chapter 2 that discusses New Britain's separation from Berlin in 1850. This account of the city's birth was based on more than 60 pages of General Assembly documents and petitions that, to the best of my knowledge, have never been reported before.

Many people have helped in the preparation of this book, and to all of them I am very thankful. I am especially thankful to the staff of the New Britain Public Library, and Arlene Palmer, curator of the library's Local History Room, for her help in solving numerous research problems, reading of the manuscript, and encouragement; the Reverend James A. Simpson, pastor of the First Church of Christ, Congregational, who took much time out of his busy schedule to share his extensive knowledge of the city's early history and enthusiasm for it; and fellow journalist Carole Burns, who carefully read and edited each chapter. Her affection, moral support, and encouragement made this work possible.
—Patrick Thibodeau

Benjamin Hawley had a love for children that was known citywide. In October 1916 Hawley gathered the neighborhood children together for an outing in his new Hudson automobile. Courtesy, Local History Room of the New Britain Public Library

1

THE BIRTH OF "NEW BRITON"

With hopes as intense as their fears, settlers from Boston and nearby towns began heading down the Connecticut River valley in search of new farmland less than two decades after the 1620 *Mayflower* expedition. The valley was the frontier of the time, inhabited by howling wolves and Indian tribes of whom little was known. Armed with muskets, the settlers first established towns along the Connecticut River and Long Island Sound. By 1645 enough people had settled along the Farmington River at a point called Tunxis Sepus (meaning "bend in the river") for the General Court of the Colony to incorporate the town, the state's first settlement away from a major waterway.

Colonial Farmington covered a large area, and out of it came the entire towns, or major parts, of Avon, Berlin, Bristol, Burlington, Plainville, Southington, and New Britain. New Britain was one of the last areas settled because it lacked favorable natural resources—it was either swampy or hilly, with rocky soil and waterways limited in their ability to drive a grist- or sawmill—but the prior settlement of the areas surrounding it would become one of the contributing factors to its development as a city. With towns surrounding it like spokes on a wheel, New Britain was naturally positioned to become a hub.

The people of Farmington, and those who would create New Britain, belonged to the dominant church of the time, the Congregational Church. The church's power over these frontier settlers was enormous. It enforced the moral code, operated the schools, and imposed by force of law a tax used to run the church. The minister was the town's first citizen. "The church was the state and the state the church as one as unani-

New Britain today hardly resembles this view of the parish in 1836. Although this print illustrates New Britain 14 years before its incorporation as a town, the roots of industry had already been established. The tallest building was Seth J. North's factory. Courtesy, Local History Room of the New Britain Public Library

mous in thought, interest and action as the body and mind of an individual man," wrote Elihu Burritt, New Britain's famed peace and human-rights activist of the 1800s. The church structured life in the wilderness, right down to Sunday's seating arrangements: the town's most prominent and important citizens sat near the front of the church.

A major concern of the colonial civil government was the safety of the new settlers. The threat of Indian attack faced by early Farmington was somewhat diminished by the 1637 Pequot War, which destroyed much of that southeastern Connecticut- based tribe. But the Mohawks of New York, who sometimes ventured east to hunt, were very much feared, and Connecticut settlers were under orders from the General Court to form militias to guard against attack. Although there were some violent incidents with Indians, there were never any out-

right attacks, and Farmington escaped the violence of King Philip's War of 1675, which killed an estimated sixteenth of New England's male settlers and many more Indians. Not as aggressive as the Mohawks were the Tunxis Indians, the tribe that inhabited Farmington. Over time, the settlers attempted to assimilate the tribe into their way of life.

Whatever danger the settlers faced from the Indians, however, the Indians fared far worse. Their numbers in Connecticut were decimated by war and by diseases unfamiliar to their immune systems; they lost their lands, and attempts to convert and educate them to a presumably superior way of life only helped to destroy their culture. The Tunxis Indians went such a route and in 1774 asked the General Assembly for permission to leave Connecticut and join another tribe in New York.

For more than 200 years after the first settlers arrived in Farmington, New Britain didn't exist as its own municipality. It was part of Farmington until 1785, when it became part of the newly formed town of Berlin. In 1850 New Britain, over the objections of many of its leading citizens, was made a town by the General Assembly. The separation was sought by Berlin residents fearful that the more populated, increasingly industrialized village of New Britain would dominate town government. New Britain's rich history, however, began long before it was even named, in a place called the "Great Swamp."

The Great Swamp was a large area of good but swampy farmland, some 1,800 acres located mostly in Berlin. The first men to settle there (in the early 1660s) were Jonathan Gilbert and Richard Beckley. Gilbert ran a tavern that was visited now and then by a man named Andrew Belcher. Belcher was a wealthy Boston merchant who fell in love with Gilbert's daughter Sarah, married her, and settled in the area. Using his talents and money, Belcher built houses and roads and eventually purchased land that ran from New Britain to what is now the boundary of Meriden. Through development, Belcher was hoping to attract more people to the area.

The town of Farmington had been interested in this area for some time. Between 1670 and 1675 the town divided up much of the land near the Mattabasset River to some 60 residents. But settlement wouldn't begin until 1686, when Richard Seymour, age 48, his wife Hannah, four children, and a group of others moved from Farmington village to the Great Swamp, settling on that land and land belonging to Belcher.

Seymour and his band built a fort of pointed logs 16 feet high near Christian Lane. Inside were some cabins and a deep well. Initially, the settlers spent their nights in the fort and posted guards. For them, and all New England settlers, the terror of King Philip's War lingered. The settlers and Mattabasset Indians who inhabited the Great Swamp were wary of each other. Men carried their guns with them, and women and children stayed near their cabins. Relations between Indians and settlers, however, remained peaceful.

Some time following the death in 1695 of the Reverend Samuel Hooker, their minister in Farmington, the Great Swamp settlers began efforts to form a separate religious society, an action that would require the approval of Farmington and the General Assembly. The need to do so was apparent. It was an eight- to 10-mile trip to the Farmington church along Indian trails through New Britain. Churchgoers would leave at dawn for the daylong service and, depending on the season, take as long as several hours to make the trip. It was a trip they were willing to make as long as Hooker lived. Men carrying loaded muskets would walk to the rear and front of the column on the lookout for Indians. In 1705 the settlers received approval to create the Second Church of Farmington, also called the Great Swamp Parish. The Reverend William Burnham of Wethersfield was selected as their minister in 1707. He became pastor in 1709, and on December 10, 1712, the day of his ordination, the church was officially organized. In 1722 the parishioners of the Great Swamp Parish, unhappy with their dubious name, successfully petitioned the General Assembly to rename Great Swamp to Kensington.

New Britain's genesis as a distinctive community took place within the present-day limits of Berlin. Out of the Great Swamp settlement, families began to settle New Britain in earnest. In 1690 Stephen Lee (grandfather of New Britain's first magistrate, Colonel Isaac Lee) was the first Great Swamp settler to construct a house in New Britain on East Street near Smalley

Street. There is evidence, however, that prior to the building of Lee's house, some people built cabins in what is now the northwest section of New Britain, not too long after the settlement of Farmington. Seymour, the man who led the Great Swamp settlement, also was the first to be buried in the Great Swamp burial grounds (Christian Lane Cemetery)—on land he donated for that very use. He died while cutting down a tree in 1710.

As new generations were born and more settlers arrived, pressure grew from the various settlements throughout the large area of Farmington to separate from the "mother" parish. New Britain's division from the Kensington Society follows such a pattern. When the original Christian Lane meeting house was eventually replaced, its new location meant a walk of an extra mile for the settlers on East Street. Soon after, in 1739, the early New Britain settlers petitioned the General Assembly for winter privileges, or permission to meet in New Britain four months out of the year. The petition was rejected and may have faced opposition from the Kensington Society because of the feared

loss of ministerial taxes. Other efforts to separate in the following years also failed. But following the death of Burnham in 1750, efforts to separate were renewed. Success came in 1754 when the General Assembly granted approval to create a new ecclesiastical society combining sections of the Kensington, Farmington, and Newington ecclesiastical societies. The Assembly decreed that the society "shall be known by the name of New Briton." Why the apparent misspelling occurred is

FACING PAGE: When he wrote his Ecclesiastical History, *Deacon Alfred Andrews gave New Britain a superb genealogical source. Started in 1858 and completed in 1867, this work gives biographical sketches of more than 1,000 members of First Church. Courtesy, Local History Room of the New Britain Public Library*

BELOW: Colonel Isaac Lee, one of New Britain's most prominent citizens, resided in this home. Built on Main Street, the dwelling remained in his family for many years. Courtesy, Local History Room of the New Britain Public Library

not known. The boundaries set in the original act weren't too different from today's city limits.

It's believed that New Britain was named by Colonel Isaac Lee, the village's magistrate for some 30 years and its chief law enforcer. Intelligent and strong, he was probably the village's best wrestler, a popular sport then.

At the time of its creation, New Britain was a village of less than 40 houses with a population of between 250 and 300 centered in three hamlets. Hart Quarter, near the Kensington parish line, was the least populated hamlet and the location of the Harts' grist mill. Stanley Quarter, in the northwest, was where Noah Stanley ran the village's first tavern, the Stanley Tavern, and where Thomas Richards, one of the first blacksmiths in New Britain, lived. East Street, the third hamlet, was the most densely populated and the center of village life.

It was a hard and self-sufficient life for these settlers. They were off the main roads of commerce, had little wealth, and did much of their business by barter. Infant mortality was high. In the oldest section of Fairview Cemetery, 23 of 85 tombstone records checked (from the mid-1750s to mid-1800s) belonged to children aged five or under, with most of the deaths occurring within the first year of life. Epidemics of typhus, cholera, and smallpox were common. From 1792 to 1794 there was a smallpox hospital in Farmington near the Southington town line, where patients, some from New Britain, were inoculated and treated by physicians without waiting for symptoms of the milder form of the disease to develop. Polly Stanley, a daughter of New Britain's Revolutionary War Colonel Gad Stanley, spent several weeks in the so-called "pest house" convalescing after her inoculation.

The early inhabitants of New Britain, like most people of those days, had large families, generally of from five to 12 children. A typical family history of the time, as recorded in Alfred Andrew's 1867 *Genealogy and Ecclesiastical History of New Britain*, concerns James and Hannah Judd. The Judds had nine children—Hannah giving birth in 1750, 1752, 1754, 1755, 1757, 1759, 1761, 1764, and 1768. One child died at three months, one at age 12, another at 19, and their firstborn at 30. Judd owned a sawmill called Judd's Mill. He died in 1783 at age 66, and Hannah died in 1789 at age 67.

The diet of the time was simple and monotonous, consisting mainly of foods raised locally—such as salt beef, mutton, pork, potatoes, turnips—plus a breakfast of eggs, potatoes, and ham. It was the custom of neighbors to butcher their animals at different times and to share their fresh meat, thus providing a somewhat steady supply. Social activities often revolved around work, such as raising a barn or house frame, quilt making, or autumn corn husking. Taverns eventually were established in all three hamlets and were popular social gathering spots, though drunkenness was a problem.

There is little record of the activities of women. They were excluded from official positions in both church and government. While in church they sat with their backs to the pulpit facing the men. Rearing children was their major occupation, and they had to be skilled in a large number of complex tasks, including making clothes, candles, and butter, preserving food, and operating a loom and spinning wheel. Some women managed the household finances, and, if their husbands died before them, their farms. Some women specialized in midwifery. A few of the village's wealthier residents owned slaves.

Preparations for the Sabbath service began on Saturday afternoon. One village resident, Elijah Hart, ended all work on his farm at 4 P.M. on Saturday. After carefully brushing his long coat and shaving, Hart, with lunch in his pocket, would walk or ride a horse with the other parishioners to Sunday's daylong service to hear the pastor they had taken great pains to pick, the Reverend John Smalley. Wearing a three-cornered cocked hat, a single-breasted black coat with metal buttons, and boots with large silver buckles, the tall and well-built Smalley usually arrived through the church's main entrance at the moment the service was to begin. Often he stomped his foot or tapped his cane on the floor to let the parishioners know that he had arrived.

In a 1960 paper on Smalley, a former First Church minister, the Reverend Edward C. Dahl, said:

With his ordination and installation behind him, Smalley became a man of no little importance in the scheme of things in colonial Connecticut. The clergy of the colony made up of the so-called "Standing Order" were a privileged group which expected and intended to govern the church and, in association with the magistrates, the state as well.

Their words and decisions were expected to have the force of law. This was quite a step up in the world for the young man who at Yale was 27th in his class of 33 in social prominence and standing . . . He was now the first citizen of the community and he expected to be listened to, deferred to, and obeyed at all times.

The men would rise, turn toward him, and bow.

Outside of Colonel Lee no person played as long or as important a role in early New Britain as Smalley. He was an exceptional individual, known for his sermons throughout New England and to some extent in England. Intelligent, tough- minded, a sharp wit, he became a successful farmer, a skilled teacher, and as much as a source of controversy as pride for New Britain.

The Yale graduate was born June 4, 1734 in Lebanon. While Smalley was at Yale, his father lost his property, and if it had not been for the help of Ezra Stiles (who would later become Yale's president), Smalley might have had to drop out. Following the creation of the Ecclesiastical Society of New Britain, the parish began work on a barn-like meeting house between East and Main streets, at about the center of the village. New Britain—rough, primitive and poor—was not an attractive place, and several earlier candidates for the post had rejected it. In 1757 Smalley accepted, and after negotiations the society agreed to pay him a one-time cash settlement of 150 pounds, then 50 pounds and 20 cords of wood a year for the first three years. His salary was increased to 60 pounds after three years. One year earlier the General Assembly had approved a ministerial tax so that the society could pay its minister. After a probationary period, Smalley was ordained in April 1758, and the First Church of Christ was officially formed.

In the years leading up to the Revolutionary War, Smalley's reputation grew. In 1769 two of his sermons on "Natural and Moral Inability" were published here and in England. Many of his works eventually were published in two volumes. As a tutor, his students included such men as Oliver Ellsworth, who in 1796 became Chief Justice of the U.S. Supreme Court; Nathaniel Emmons, later to become a leading theologian of the day; and Ebenezer Porter, later president of Andover Theological Seminary. There can be no doubt that Smalley was an equally excellent counsel to his parishioners. Like other ministers of his day, he didn't confine his sermons to theological issues and often discussed politics, a subject very much on the minds of the New Britain residents. In 1770 residents of Farmington (including New Britain) voted against the purchase of imported goods as a protest against colonial government policies. When the British blocked the port of Boston, residents voted on June 15, 1774, to send wheat, rye, Indian corn, and other provisions in relief.

During a time when many Connecticut ministers were supporting resistance, Smalley was taking a minority view favoring conservative approaches to problems with the British. Smalley has been labeled over time as a loyalist to colonial rule. This may be unfair. The incident that has tarnished Smalley's reputation occurred on September 4, 1774, when news reached New Britain that Boston was under siege. The news came on a Sunday, and Colonel Lee gave notice in the church, immediately following the service, that a meeting would be held that night. That announcement—in church—apparently inflamed Smalley. "It was like throwing down the glove of defiance to his opinion and authority at the foot of the pulpit," wrote Burritt. While the parishioners excitedly discussed the events just outside the church, Smalley came out the door and said, "What! Will you fight your king?" For those parishioners, who would vote as a town on September 20 to buy a large quantity of lead, flint, and gunpowder for that very purpose, Smalley's statement caused considerable uproar. Another man shot back to Smalley, "Yes! And I would shoot him as though he were a blacksnake." Colonel Lee managed to calm tempers down, but the incident ignited apparently long-simmering resentment

ABOVE: Ordained as New Britain's first pastor, the Reverend John Smalley served his parish for 62 years, 50 as pastor and 12 more as pastor emeritus. In spite of his severe and rather austere manner, Smalley was considered the absolute authority by his congregation. Courtesy, Local History Room of the New Britain Public Library

LEFT: The Reverend John Smalley often wrote his sermons out in longhand on small pieces of paper. A packet of these sermons is among the oldest items of the parish still in existence. These are housed in the Local History Room of the New Britain Public Library. Courtesy, Local History Room of the New Britain Public Library

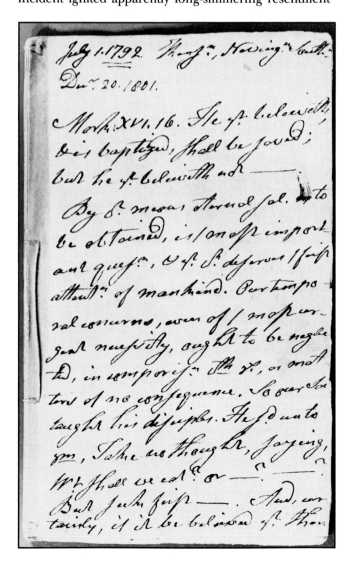

against Smalley's views. Smalley, who may have received threats from some members of the Sons of Liberty in Farmington, rode to Bethlehem to seek the help of the Reverend Joseph Bellamy, who was his tutor after he left Yale. Bellamy went to New Britain to preach for Smalley and restore peace. It wasn't enough. In the October 10 edition of the *Connecticut Courant* (now the *Hartford Courant*), a lengthy letter by Smalley was published.

As to measures proper taken by us [Smalley wrote], I have been much for moderate measures, I confess. However, I am not for submitting tamely to a yoke of bondage, that neither we nor our children will be able to bear. I am not for suffering the chains of slavery to be fastened on our necks, and on the necks of unborn posterity, without resistance or opposition. I have always been in favor of the proposed non importation and non consumption agreements, and with, if there is occasion, and can be time for measures of this kind to operate, they may still be carried into execution with greater unanimity. And if we are driven to it by dire necessity, and there is a rational prospect of being able to defend ourselves in this and in no other way, we must have recourse to arms.

Smalley, obviously humbled, closed his letter by saying that if he had inadvertently said anything that was inconsistent with these sentiments, "I disapprove and retract it." Following Smalley's letter was another letter signed by 58 of the male members of the New Britain society, saying that the "above retraction . . . gives us full and complete satisfaction." Colonel Lee's name is absent from that letter. In the following week's issue of the *Courant*, the Sons of Liberty responded, along with a number of other letters from people who witnessed Smalley's statement at the church, and complained of past positions by Smalley. One letter writer said that Smalley had called the Stamp Act "but a trifling thing." Smalley stirred up more ill will in 1775 when he read a proclamation for a special fast day declared by the Continental Congress, but told his parishioners that Congress had no power over them and that they were under no obligation to observe it.

No Revolutionary War battles were fought in New Britain. There are 29 Revolutionary War veterans in Fairview Cemetery, although records indicate that between 1775 and 1783, about 90 New Britain men served in the American Army. Among those were Brigadier General John Patterson, an early New Britain resident and friend of George Washington. Patterson fought at Trenton, Princeton, and Saratoga, where he participated in the capture of the British force of General John Burgoyne and his army of 5,000. Gad Stanley, a captain in the local militia, won fame when

Born in New Britain in 1744 and educated at Yale University, Brigadier General John Patterson would serve his town and country well. He fought in the Battle of Lexington and was with George Washington at the Delaware Crossing. In 1780 he was in command of West Point and was made a major general in 1783. He died in 1808, and was buried in Lenox, Massachusetts. Courtesy, Herald photo files

he led his men to safety during the battle of Long Island, while others retreating were less successful. Among those who fought were the six sons of Moses and Lydia Andrews. Their youngest son, aged 16, enlisted after the oldest one, aged 27, was killed. When Seth Judd was killed by an accidental gun discharge, his uncle, Captain Phineas Judd, enlisted. He was 62.

New Britain would remain largely a farming community until well into the early 1800s. By 1800 its population had reached about 950, and by 1830 had increased only to about 1,200. Many of its residents lived and died without venturing far from New Britain's borders. No post office was established until 1825. The community eventually was divided into six school districts, with classes in one-room schoolhouses or in portions of private residences. Its roads were little more than cow paths, and in the winter children sometimes were brought to school on sleds drawn by cattle. Main Street eventually would replace East Street as the village's principal thoroughfare, but aside from those two streets, New Britain's land was over- whelmingly devoted to farming. In the area from Broad to Burritt streets, now a busy commercial and residential strip, there were no buildings. By the mid-1820s there were fewer than 20 buildings on Main Street, including a tannery, a pound used to hold stray sheep and cattle, a shoe shop, a shop manufacturing brass goods, several other black- smith shops or small manufacturers, a cider mill, a schoolhouse, and a store. Next to the pound was a whipping post where people convicted of minor crimes were punished. One eyewitness account tells of a father and son who were found guilty of stealing

ABOVE: Referred to as the "Skinner House," this structure from the 1750s belonged to Josiah Lee. Lee's daughter married Revolutionary War hero John Patterson at the house in 1766. The Lees sold the home to a blacksmith, John Richards, who in turn sold it to the Reverend Newton Skinner, second pastor of the First Church. Skinner remained here until his death. Courtesy, Local History Room of the New Britain Public Library

BELOW: The 150th anniversary of the founding of First Church was celebrated in 1908. This boulder unveiling commemorated the event. The boulder was eventually moved from the site of the first meeting house to Smalley School, and in recent years moved again to the grounds of the present site of the First Church on Corbin Avenue. Courtesy, Herald *photo files*

clothes from a line and were each sentenced to 10 lashes on their bare backs. About 30 watched the punishment.

New Britain, nevertheless, was changing in the early 1800s. The Congregational Church's power to tax was ended by the General Assembly in 1818. New churches were being established. The First Baptist Church was organized in 1808, and what is believed to be the first Methodist sermon in New Britain was delivered in 1815. A new First Church was constructed in 1822.

Smalley died in 1820 at age 86. In 1800 he received a doctorate from the College of New Jersey, which later became Princeton University. When he proposed retiring at the age of 70 in 1804, his parishioners talked him out of it. In 1809 a successor, the Reverend Newton Skinner of Granby, was appointed to replace Smalley, who continued to preach occasionally until 1813. He and his first wife raised six daughters, and over the course of his life he built up a large estate. Smalley's last articulate words, according to Burritt, were, "I believe I was right." Only Smalley knows what he meant.

2

DEVELOPMENT

AND CITYHOOD

In 1874 Frederick T. Stanley, the city's first mayor, was 72 and entering the last decade of his life. It was a time of reflection for him. Using stationery bearing the name of the company he had founded, the Stanley Works, he wrote of the city's early manufacturing history and offered his reasons why small, landlocked New Britain—a village once without significant wealth and away from the main roads of commerce—had developed into the manufacturing center it had become: a city, unbeknownst to Stanley, on the verge of becoming the hardware capital of the world. The city's success, Stanley believed, was largely due to the earlier efforts of one person: Seth J. North, a man he called the "father and founder" of New Britain.

North is an enigmatic, but now virtually forgotten figure in the city's history. Although he never held elected office, he was as much the village's leader as Stanley was as mayor. Few business or civic ventures were undertaken without North's money or consent. His early business successes gave him the money to buy up large tracts of the village's farmland at bargain prices, and at the time of his death in 1851 he was considered one of the wealthiest men in Hartford County. North's most enduring legacy was the effort he led, in the last years of his life, to convince the state to locate its first teacher training school in New Britain—the Normal School, known today as Central Connecticut State University. A number of communities also wanted that school, but North engineered a financial package superior to those of other towns. For those who knew North, his success in getting the school for the city was not surprising. Beating out competitors was something North had spent his life doing.

North was born in 1779, one of four sons of James North. His father was an intelligent and talented

One of the city's largest parks, Walnut Hill, offered an overview of the city that is as striking today as it was when this photograph was taken in about 1898. Courtesy, Local History Room of the New Britain Public Library

LEFT: Frederick T. Stanley typifies the ingenuity of New Britain. Born in Stanley Quarter in 1802, he spent time in North Carolina engaged in business before returning home to found one of the greatest hardware industries in the nation: the Stanley Works. He manufactured the first locks in the country and then expanded into other areas of hardware. Stanley was also civic-minded, acting as the borough's first warden and then the city's first mayor in 1871. Courtesy, Local History Room of the New Britain Public Library

FACING PAGE, TOP: Sometimes called the "Father of New Britain," Seth North was a powerful influence in early New Britain. He began his career as a blacksmith, became a leading industrialist, and was primarily responsible for the organization of the South Congregational Church. Courtesy, Local History Room of the New Britain Public Library

FACING PAGE, BOTTOM: The North brothers began a brass business in 1812 that would undergo several changes in partners before incorporating as North and Judd in 1863. Brass products were considered among the first items manufactured in New Britain. Courtesy, Local History Room of the New Britain Public Library

man who wanted a better life for his children. James North, born in 1748, was only 10 when his father died. As a youth he learned his trade in the blacksmith shop of John Richards of Stanley Quarter. He became one of the better blacksmiths in New Britain, capable of making a large variety of specialized tools and household wares used by village farmers. He also made some brass goods, like shoe buckles and andirons, in his West Main Street shop. By 1800 the elder North had become a pillar of the church and represented the town in the state General Assembly. He owned more than 60 acres of land, and his family possessed two of the 14 silver watches owned in the New Britain parish, according to an 1800 census. The only gold watches were those owned by residents living in the Kensington and Worthington sections of Berlin.

James North was no doubt aware of the successful manufacturing business started by two Scotsmen some time after 1740, when they arrived in Kensington. William and Edward Patterson (also spelled Pattison) imported tin sheets from England and began manufacturing tinware, the first in America to do so. Most of what they produced was kitchenware, and their products soon became popular. Tinware was light, easy to use, and clean, and was considered superior to the wood, earthenware, and pewter then in common use. At first the Pattersons sold their products door-to-door in the immediate area. In time, as others copied the Patterson's success, a number of men began to specialize in selling it. Initially they used handcarts,

and later horse-drawn wagons, to carry their products to neighboring villages. These new products, except during the Revolutionary War when imports were suspended, gradually were spread throughout the country by salesmen later known as "yankee peddlers."

By the close of the 1700s, tinware was being manufactured throughout the region, including New Britain. It was a profitable, but by then competitive business. James North knew from his own work that he could make a profit manufacturing products from metals other than tin, but his skills were rudimentary. He met with some neighbors and discussed sending his eldest son, James North, Jr., and other young men from the village to Stockbridge, Massachusetts, to learn the brass business from Joseph Barton. Two other families agreed.

In 1799 the younger North, Joseph Shipman, and Joseph Booth returned from Stockbridge. North and Shipman went into business together and began manufacturing brass sleigh bells on property near what is now Park and South Main streets, while Booth moved to New York with his parents. The joint effort of North and Shipman is believed by city historians to be the beginning of New Britain's industrial development. Within a year of their venture, North and Shipman went their separate ways. The Reverend Smalley, who had a reputation for prudence and conservatism in financial matters, lent Shipman $50 for his venture. Shipman continued making sleigh bells and other brass goods (furniture, house fittings) at his father's joiner shop until it burned down in 1803. He then built his own shop on Stanley

Street, and his brass foundry business continued successfully and expanded, until the financial panic of 1837 closed it along with many other businesses.

James North, Jr., left New Britain in 1803 for Cherry Valley, New York, and his business went to his brother Seth, who had been working with him. Years later North returned to New Britain and died in 1825. His father died in 1833. In the years to follow, Shipman's and Seth North's shops would be the two principal brass foundries in town. They, and the others in the village who would take up manufacturing in later years, had some advantages that contributed to their success. Most of the items they produced from 1800 to 1830 were small—jewelry, hooks and eyes used for clothing, small hardware items, buckles, coat clasps, and other metal products—and could be carried easily by the yankee peddlers along their well-established routes. While New Britain may have seemed isolated to its residents, its manufacturers weren't far from the ports of New York and Boston, sources of raw materials.

Prior to the advent of manufacturing, the economy was based on what the farm produced. The modest manufacturing efforts of the early 1800s gradually worked to increase the amount of wealth and capital in the community, money that was reinvested in new operations. Many of these early manufacturing efforts were small—employing no more than one or two persons—and work was done by hand. Partnerships were formed and dissolved with some frequency. Women and children often were employed to assemble or make parts in their homes.

While North maintained his brass foundry business, he branched out in other areas. In 1812 North, his brother Alvin, and Hezekiah C. Whipple began a "plating business," producing silver plated buckles, coat clasps, and eventually plated saddle hardware. Out of that partnership, the North & Judd Manufacturing Company, incorporated in 1863, evolved.

In 1829 North, in partnership with others, built a four-story factory to manufacture hardware. It was the largest in town, and the first to use horsepower on a regular basis to drive machinery. In 1831 Frederick T. Stanley started New Britain's first lock manufacturing com- pany, the F.T. Stanley Company. In 1832 Stanley bought a steam engine to use in manufacturing—the first in town. He was involved in several other manufacturing ventures until 1842, when he began manufacturing bolts and hinges, setting the foundation for the Stanley Works—the last of the surviving manufacturing giants to be formed in the middle 1800s—which are still in business today in New Britain.

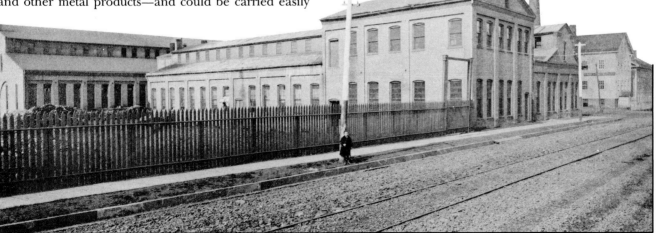

Manufacturers got little help from local government prior to 1850, the year New Britain was incorporated. Until then the roads remained little more than muddy paths, with drainage ranging from poor to nonexistent. The ability of volunteers for the local fire department, which had been organized in the mid-1830s, depended on how quickly they could scoop water out of the Lock Shop Pond (a downtown pond that was paved over and drained in the twentieth century). Most of the early village improvements were the result of efforts of people like North, who constructed Elm Street (the first straight road in the village) and a canal from Lock Shop Pond to supply his brick factory with waterpower.

The villagers, however, seemed more content

By 1830 North had become prosperous, and his prestige had been established. A major in the local militia, he continued to be addressed by his military title until his death. He was never a person to stay with one type of business activity, and his diversification had its advantages. A Waterbury firm that had been supplying him with the copper wire he needed for his hook-and-eye business (he plated the wire with silver) saw the profits North was making and decided to go into the same business. In an attempt to put North out of business, the firm increased the cost of the wire. North responded by making 250,000 bricks in the brick factory he owned. He told the Waterbury firm that if they didn't sell him the wire at a fair cost, he was going to use the bricks to build his own wire mill. The Waterbury company backed down, and North later, in 1847, used the bricks to build the New Britain Knitting Company with two other partners.

If North's effort to keep the hook-and-eye business seemed extraordinary, consider what he did to get it. Some time prior to the Waterbury incident, North had been involved with his brother Henry in making hooks and eyes, according to a paper written in 1888 by Charles Peck, himself a manufacturer. Although Henry had purchased equipment invented in Hartford to speed production, North urged his brother to improve the production method even more. Henry refused, so North hired two of the best mechanics in town, who improved the machinery until it was nearly automatic. At about the same time that Seth North started his own hook-and-eye business, another North brother, Alvin, seeing the large profits in the business, decided to manufacture hooks and eyes also. The competition between the three brothers, and others in the village making hooks and eyes, was intense. Determined to control the market, North undercut everyone, and the businesses were consolidated under his control.

ABOVE: Mortimer D. Stanley's store was located on the south side of Church Street between Elm and the railroad tracks. Like other stores of the time, he carried a variety of goods, from flour to hardware. Courtesy, Local History Room of the New Britain Public Library

BELOW: School rooms were sparse, yet geared toward learning, in the early twentieth century. Miss Kempf, a teacher at East Street School, poses in her classroom in 1903. Courtesy, Local History Room of the New Britain Public Library

with barely existing municipal services then they were
with the school system. By the 1830s there was general dis-
satisfaction with the school district and the quality of
teachers, spurring a number of residents to form private schools. Many of these efforts were supported by
North and his brothers. One such school was the
"Academy," created in the late 1820s and used to provide college preparatory training for those few students
who could attend college. One of the earliest efforts in
the state to improve the quality of teachers was undertaken in New Britain. In 1838 the village raised $4,000
to establish a county school for training teachers.

For many years prior to the state's authorization
of the Normal School in 1849, state legislators had debated its need. Pressure for a teacher training facility
had been growing throughout the state, and ultimately
public demand convinced the General Assembly to
move forward. The state's approval came with the stipula-
tion that the town receiving the facility had to provide
the building and furnishings. In addition to New Britain, the towns of Middletown, Farmington, and Southington also were interested in the school. After donating
$6,000 toward the project, North led a fund drive con-
vincing 99 others to contribute, and $16,250 was raised.
A recently completed town hall in the village would
instead be used for the Normal School. New Britain's
package was the best, and it was selected as the site
for the state's first Normal School.

Support for the Normal School was not unanimous.
The *Hartford Times,* in an 1850 editorial, called the
school "humbug, calculated to burden your state treas-
ury." It believed "demand" would "supply" teachers. It
didn't suggest where the supply would come from. In
1867 the Normal School was closed by the General
Assembly for two years as a way to cut post-Civil War
debt. In 1881 the state approved $75,000 for a new
Normal School building, provided that New Britain contribute $25,000. It did, and in 1883 the building was
constructed at 27 Hillside Place. The town hall was

never replaced. Town, and later city, business would be conducted in a number of private buildings until 1907, when the Russwin Hotel was purchased and converted into City Hall.

The school also served as catalyst for other educational improvements. In 1850 New Britain established a high school, also housed in the Normal School building. It was one of the first free public high schools in the state. The school districts were consolidated, and a "model school" was established in the Normal School. A system of grades also was created.

The school system and later municipal improvements were needed because of the village's growing manufacturing and population. The population, which had been slow to grow until 1840, was rising rapidly as midcentury approached. Attracted by factory work, Irish and German immigrants were becoming a larger part of New Britain. The increases may have been spurred by railway development. In 1839 the Hartford and New Haven Railroad was opened with a station located in Newington, about one-and-a-half miles from New Britain. North was a director of the railroad and had tried to have it routed through the village, but Meriden officials, together with Kensington and Worthington residents, were able to get the route designed in a way that favored them. Meriden, especially, was larger and more economically developed then New Britain at the time. In 1850 New Britain got direct railroad service when the Hartford-Providence line was extended through the village. The railroad was opposed by some farmers, who saw it cheapening the value of their horses and farmland.

In 1830 the estimated population of the three parishes that made up Berlin (Kensington, Worthington, and New Britain) was 3,037. By 1850 it had only increased to 3,411. But by 1850 the population of Berlin increased to about 4,900, with two-thirds of the approximately 1,500 new arrivals settling in New Britain. The population increase gave New Britain residents new political muscle, which they used over Kensington and Worthington parishes with severe consequences for themselves.

Following the separation of Berlin from Farmington in 1785, town meetings were held on a rotating basis in the three parishes, usually in a church meetinghouse. In 1845 the residents of all three parishes voted to build a town hall in the "geographical center" of town. In 1846, however, that resolution was rescinded

by the voting strength of New Britain citizens, who followed with another vote in 1848 to locate the proposed town hall in their village. That action prompted Kensington residents to petition the General Assembly in 1850 for approval to separate from Worthington and New Britain, forming a town "to be called by the name of Kensington," according to General Assembly records. Worthington residents objected to Kensington's plan and petitioned the General Assembly, meeting in New Haven that year, for approval to separate Worthington and Kensington parishes from New Britain. They argued that if Kensington residents were granted their wish, Worthington would be connected to New Britain by only a small section of land in New Britain's southeastern corner. Moreover, Worthington citizens would have to travel four to six miles through Kensington to vote at their town hall in New Britain. There are no General Assembly records indicating how New Britain residents felt about the proposed division; David N. Camp's *History of New Britain*, however, states that several of New Britain's leading citizens went to the General Assembly to speak in opposition to the proposed division. If so, their arguments were not recorded.

Some New Britain residents also wanted changes in local government in 1850, but not as drastic as what was being sought by Kensington and Worthington. These residents—merchants and factory owners living in the village's downtown, led by North—petitioned the legislature for approval to incorporate most of downtown as a borough. The borough would remain part of Berlin, but it would be administered independently, with the power to levy taxes for public improvements business leaders felt were now very necessary. By 1850 "the greater portion" of the village's population was "engaged in manufacturing pursuits and in the mechanical arts, and that within the limits of said society (New Britain is estimated one of the most extensive manufacturing villages in said state)," they said in their petition. That self-assessment of their community was, in some respects, complimented in 1851 by the *Hartford Times,* which described New Britain as "one of the most thrifty towns in the state. It can boast some of the energetic men and the most enterprising capitalists and mechanics. They never surrender, but put everything through that they undertake. It is a moral, well-regulated community."

The General Assembly approved New Britain's request to create a borough, along with the division of the Kensington and Worthington societies from New Britain. New Britain was now a town and borough, and Kensington and Worthington the town of Berlin. The legislature's Joint Standing Committee on Towns and Probate Districts, in its report recommending the di-

vision, cited the arguments raised by Worthington and Kensington residents. In addition to having to travel "long and unnecessary distances" to attend town meetings, Kensington and Worthington paid more than one-half of the town's taxes, while making up only two-fifths of the population. According to the 1849 grand list, the total value of all taxable property in New Britain was $26,911, less than the combined grand list of Kensington ($11,163) and Worthington ($17,849). A minority report, filed by members of the same legislative committee, said they believed it was unjust for "a minority of the population and Worthington– to be set-off and constituted a new town," and that the "facts" concerning the problems are chiefly a "state of feelings" that are "excited by no sufficient grounds." The General Assembly ordered the new towns to divide their assets. New Britain was allowed to keep the town-meeting and property records. Berlin residents felt that those records rightly belonged to them and made at least two efforts over many decades to have them returned. It wouldn't be until the mid-1970s that the General Assembly authorized their return.

Following New Britain's incorporation, town and

borough officials began public-works projects for improvement of roads, drainage, schools, police, and fire protection, and for construction of a lock-up, or jail. The need for water for firefighting and manufacturing led to the creation of "the water works." Stanley, who was the borough's first warden as well as its first mayor, organized the effort to turn Shuttle Meadow from a swamp into a reservoir by constructing a dam. When the project was completed in 1857, and piping was laid, a fountain that gushed water to treetop level was installed in Central Park. It was believed to be the largest fountain in the state and was a source of community pride.

The political problems of the 1840s were just one part of the turmoil in New Britain during that period. In the 30 years prior to the outbreak of the Civil War in 1861, New Britain residents were divided—sometimes violently—over abolition and temperance. These issues would lead to the split of the church that had been the community's bedrock, First Church.

Throughout the 1830s in New England, there was a growing antislavery movement. The New England Anti-Slavery Society became a national organization two years after its formation in 1831, the year Nat Turner led his violent insurrection in Virginia. By 1830 there were no slaves in Hartford County and only a few New Britain families had ever owned slaves since the society was incorporated in 1754. But that did not lessen the issue's importance.

The clear division in New Britain over abolition reached an acute level in the church because it was there that abolitionists wanted the issue discussed—and endorsed. But the movement faced opposition in the North for number of reasons, including racism and beliefs that abolition was a threat to the union and a challenge to the rights of states.

When the Reverend Dwight M. Seward was hired in 1835 to fill a vacancy at First Church, he no doubt was aware of the issues of the day. But seven years after a committee of the church, which included North, had given him the nod for the job, Seward would resign, his parish divided beyond hope and his health ruined. At the close of his ministry in New Britain, he would write: "Contentions, it is true, have prevailed among this people for many years, but the subjects to which they formerly pertained have in great measure given place to others; while in one spot the wounds have appeared to be rapidly healing, they have violently broken out in another." Meetings were held, committees appointed, compromises proposed, "all apparently to no avail," said Seward. In July 1842, 120 members, about one-third of the membership of First Church, received approval from the church's governing body, the South Consocation of Hartford, to form South Congregational Church. Among them was North, who had been on the committee that hired Seward.

The consociation's approval of the division was a foregone conclusion as far as North was concerned. He, and his brothers Alvin and Henry, had donated half of the new church's $8,000 construction cost one year earlier. South Church was completed in the spring of 1842, several months before the consociation took its action.

Some evidence of the dividing issues is found in resolutions passed by First Church members. In 1837 a resolution was approved stating that "as a church we consider the manufacturing, vending or using as drink spiritus liquor, to be contrary to the spirit of the Gospel and a gross immorality." While the resolution was strongly worded, it concluded by only "recommending" abstinence. That 1837 resolution may have been a compromise because in 1843, one year after the division, the remaining First Church members passed a new resolution saying that any church member who didn't "conform strictly" to the principles of the temperance movement wouldn't be considered a suitable candidate for church membership.

Parishioners who were "in the habit of intemperate use of ardent spirits," and using "profane language" (the two charges usually went together) could be brought before the congregation and made to make a public confession, in which they promised to change their ways or face expulsion. The various temperance movements during that period, like the "Cold Water Army," were sweeping through New Britain, and a number of parishioners joined, signing pledges not to drink. Some were affected in other ways by the movement, like Amon Stanley (1778-1846) who distilled cider brandy in the village. His wife had reservations about the business, so Amon sold it to others who continued it. That apparently bothered him or his wife, because

he later repurchased the distillery and destroyed it.

At the same 1843 meeting that approved the stricter temperance resolution, First Church members also passed a resolution condemning slavery. The resolution said, "we deem it our duty as a church . . . to protest against the entire system in the spirit of the gospel, to use all suitable means for its suppression." It was no idle resolution. Of the 22 agents for the Underground Railroad in Hartford County listed in Horatio T. Strother's *The Underground Railroad in Connecticut,* nine of them were New Britain residents; of the nine, eight were members of First Church. The exception was Henry North, who belonged to South Congregational Church.

Protesting abolition was a dangerous activity. Camp makes mention of two men, Isaac Botsford (1786-1851) and Milo Hotchkiss (1802-1874), both of Berlin, who suffered because of their antislavery activities. Botsford, a farmer and manufacturer, lost money in his business, and Hotchkiss, a portrait painter who was also active in the temperance movement, suffered "in person and property from attacks of opponents of these causes." Charles Peck relates how one New Britain abolition meeting was mobbed by opponents throwing rotten eggs. Another time, a cannon on Walnut Hill was brought near an abolitionist meeting and fired off "at intervals" in an attempt to disrupt it. One of the earliest and most ardent abolitionists in New Britain was a woman, Minerva Hart, who was once mobbed, along with her husband, for their antislavery activities. On one October night in 1857, arsonists torched barns belonging to Henry North and Horace Booth, also an abolitionist. In 1861 the builders of a Court Street house hid a tablet in the walls that said the building was being constructed at a time when "the damnable doctrine of Negro Slavery" was being used to "perpetuate the reign of a Cotton Aristocracy." The tablet was discovered when the house was demolished in 1930. One group in town opposing the cause was the "Free Soil" movement, which believed that Southern states should be allowed to continue slavery but no new states allowed to institute it.

In addition to the abolitionist and temperance issues, theological issues also divided the church. Twenty-three years after the split, when church historian Alfred Andrews (who was an agent for the Underground Railroad) wrote his ecclesiastical history of New Britain, he discussed the issues that divided the church. "We look back with wonder," he said, "that so slight causes should have produced so great a breach. Indeed we are forced to look for other more potent causes, and on the above as mere occasions for greater causes to operate." Andrews didn't speculate on what the underlying causes might be.

The underlying reasons for the church split may have been related to the community's business interests. Southern states were very important to New Britain for the sale of both goods and raw materials. City and company histories frequently mention manufacturers' traveling to Southern states to conduct business. When the secession of the Southern states occurred, Russell & Erwin, one of New Britain's largest manufacturers, lost $100,000 owed by Southern merchants. The families who joined South Church in the years after the split were, like the Norths, among the wealthiest in the community and its leading manufacturers: F.T. Stanley, Cornelius B. Erwin (1811-1885) of the firm Russell & Erwin, Philip Corbin (1824-1910) of P. & F. Corbin, and Henry Stanley (1807-1884) of North and Stanley (with Alvin North). Many of these manufacturers had marital as well as business ties. Connecticut depended heavily on cotton goods for its mills, and slaves were important to cotton production. It's not certain where North fell in the issues of the time. One biographer, writing for the *American Journal of Education* eight years after North's death, included this statement about him: "He was not a bigot; not perhaps as outwardly zealous a professor as some."

Whatever fears New Britain manufacturers may have had about the increasing strain between the North and South and its impact on business were ultimately unfounded. The Civil War, instead of having a ruinous effect, had just the opposite impact. Nearly every factory in the city got federal contracts to make defense-related goods. Second and third shifts were added to meet production demands. The population of New Britain nearly doubled, from 5,212 in 1860 to 9,480 in 1870. The Stanley Works, which in 1860 reported annual sales of $53,000, posted sales of $480,000 in 1872. New Britain manufacturers made cavalry equipment, bayonets, and other military hardware items. The manufacturers "almost without exception made a good deal of money and with the earnings they developed their lines of business, increased the size of their plants and the town grew quite rapidly," wrote Andrew Jackson Sloper, a banker, in a 1916 paper. In 1866 the *New Britain Record,* a newspaper, said there were at least 100 men employed in New Britain "whose families are in other places because not a tenement can be secured for them." Existing housing was overcrowded, and the *Record* called for the construction of 200 new houses. The demand for housing also sharply increased real estate prices, and wages were said to be at their highest levels. By 1860 New Britain was positioned to benefit from federal needs. Its manufacturing base was well-established by then, and it had railway links to major cities (some 12 trains ran daily to Hartford). New Britain was no longer isolated; it was centrally located. But the prosperity caused by the Civil War came with a price.

On April 14, 1861, a few hours after Fort Sumter was evacuated, marking the outbreak of the Civil War, a large crowd gathered at First Church. Valentine B. Chamberlain, publisher of the short-lived *New Britain*

News, gave a speech on the coming war. Behind him was a portrait of Major Anderson, Fort Sumter's commander, enclosed in a laurel wreath. Enlistments to join the Army were taken, and the first to do so, Frank E. Stanley, was killed in action at Irish Bend, Louisiana. Most of the 75 New Britain residents who died weren't killed in battle, however. Albert F. Domizio, in his book, *New Britain and The Civil War*, lists eight men who died in Civil War prison camps, 16 killed in action, 11 from wounds received in action, and 40 who died while in service, many from disease—fever, diarrhea, and in the case of one man, exhaustion on a march. The *Record* published a listing of the "Noble Dead" in 1866. As the war dragged on and its glory receded, bounties were needed to attract recruits. A three-year enlistment paid a $990 bounty—$390 from the state, and $300 each from the town and federal governments. In 1864 another New Britain newspaper, the *True Citizen*, editorialized that it hoped with the bounties there will now be found men "who will now give way to impulses of patriotism, and go fight her battles. We have long regretted the lack of patriotism which has prevailed so generally, and the unmanly trembling and effort to escape the draft by men able-bodied."

The draft could be avoided for money. The war spawned men called bounty brokers, who got large fees to find substitutes for Union Army draftees. It was a detested occupation. Henry Cadwell was one such broker.

Cadwell had been drinking in a New Britain saloon when a factory worker named Charlie Gilbert, who was playing cards with a group of friends, called him over. Gilbert took him aside and told Cadwell where a "sub" might be found. The two left the Main Street bar. Cadwell was carrying a satchel. In the early morning light the next day, Cadwell's body was found against a tree, his head split open by an ax. As word

of the discovery spread, work stopped in many New Britain factories, including Gilbert's, as employees went out to view the body. Gilbert, who had arrived late for work, looked nervous and didn't leave the shop. Gilbert was later convicted of Cadwell's murder on circumstantial evidence and sentenced to life in prison. In 1878, as Gilbert's father lay dying, it was said that he confessed to the murder. The story was believed by some, because as news of the confession spread through town, "a stranger" committed suicide in the woods. Some saw a connection between the suicide and the elder Gilbert's confession. Could the stranger have been the real killer, or an accomplice? The authorities saw no connection and didn't believe the alleged confession. In 1910 an old satchel was discovered by a man digging in his back yard in the city. He burned it along with some other things. While raking through the charred remains he found a $10 gold coin dated three years before Cadwell's death.

The longest surviving New Britain Civil War veteran was Dr. Thomas Mulligan, who died in 1936 at the age of 95. He was a highly regarded doctor, who got considerable public attention in 1908 when he revived a 60-year-old woman thought to be dead for two hours, by jolting her with electricity from batteries. It was, coincidentally, the year the first movie version of "Frankenstein" was released.

As New Britain developed as both a manufacturing community and an important educational center, its social life became more complex. Debates and lec-

tures on a wide variety of topics were common forms of entertainment. The Academy was originally used in large part for that purpose. In 1836 the New Britain Lyceum, which had an active lecture program and library, was created. The numerous choirs in town were organized into the Philharmonic Society of New Britain in 1859. In 1853 the New Britain Institute was established and charged fees for book loans. An interesting note to the town's intellectual life was the publication of a newspaper called the *Shepherdess.* Created and operated entirely by women, it was published for about two years in the early 1830s. A surviving copy includes articles about "Composition and General Reading," the nature of "Envy," and the planet Saturn. It was the first newpaper published in New Britain.

In 1847 the Phoenix Wicket Club of New Britain was organized. "Wicket" was the Yankee name for the English sport of "cricket." The matches between other communities were popular spectator events. For those who needed something more exciting than wicket, there was Seth J. North, who fitted out about six men in 1849 and sent them to California during the Gold Rush. Baseball was established on a regular organized basis in 1866, by returning Civil War veterans exposed to the sport. In 1851 the *New Britain Journal and Chronicle* carried an advertisement announcing the pending arrival of "The American Museum and Menagerie of P.T. Barnum," featuring, among other things, the 19-year-old, 15-pound, 28-inch-high "General Tom Thumb."

Evidence of New Britain's growing manufacturing prosperity was displayed in housing construction. Houses, described in one newspaper account of the late 1860s as "beautiful," and "substantial," were being constructed at a cost of between $25,000 and $50,000. Those prices were well out of reach of the average working person—with males making between $1 and $1.50 a day at that time, and women and children earning less. The earliest record of a labor action in New Britain was reported in 1859. "Moulders" employed at various factories staged a two-and-a-half-day strike in protest against an agreement among city employers not to hire moulders who had left other factories without the consent of their employers. The employers backed down from the agreement. Elihu Burritt, in his newspaper, *North & South,* called the strike a period of "very unusual excitement." In 1866 an organization calling itself the "Ten Hour League" sought to have the workday at the New Britain Knitting Company reduced from 11 to 10 hours, but a workday as long as 14 hours was not unusual. The workers faced other problems. Paid monthly, they often ran up charge accounts at stores for groceries and liquor. In return for credit, the store owner got an assignment on his or her wages. The cost of these goods often were unfairly high. On paydays the wagons of store owners would line up at factory gates seeking to collect the wages. More often then not, many workers got little or nothing after store credit was deducted. Meanwhile, the community's more affluent were being urged, in regular advertisements in the early 1870s in the *New Britain Independent,* to shop at the "Lord and Taylor" store in New York City. Some workers, living in factory-owned tenements, had the cost of housing deducted from their paychecks. State law allowed the employment of children under 14 provided that they received 60 days of schooling per year. No child under 15 was allowed to work more than 58 hours a week. There was no day care. It would be many years before conditions improved. In 1887, in an essay published by the Bureau of State Labor Statistics, New Britain State Representative Thomas H. Kehoe poignantly described the problems faced by the laboring man

who in the midst of all this material progress, is condemned to incessant toil, whose wages for long hours of laborious work are insufficient to provide his family with the bare necessaries of life, to say nothing of the luxuries; who is forced to send his wife and children into the factory to assist in supporting the family; whose wages are constantly growing less; whose employment is becoming more precarious, and at whose fireside sits poverty, grim and gaunt, asks why it is that he is not a sharer in gains of this advancing civilization.

Kehoe also was editor of the *New Britain Independent* and president of the state chapter of the Knights of Labor, a labor group which sought to solve labor problems without resorting to strikes.

This was the city of which F.T. Stanley had become mayor in 1871, a city created by a margin of one vote. The borough charter was considered inadequate

to meet the municipal needs of rapidly growing New Britain. The proposed city charter was opposed not so much because of its plans for city services, but because it would establish ward voting lines that Democrats thought favored the Republicans. There also was a debate as to how far the city lines should be extended and whether the new areas included within the city limits (not all of the town of New Britain was initially included within city boundaries) would have to pay costs toward retiring previous bonded debt. "City privileges or city taxes?" was the question of the day. When the vote was held on the city charter in January 1871, 521 voted "yes," and 520 "no." Two ballots were rejected by the election moderator because they were folded closely together, reported the *Independent.* It didn't say how the vote was cast on those rejected ballots.

F.T. Stanley, a Republican, was elected mayor on April 10, 1871. The first meeting of the Common Council was on the third Wednesday of April of that year. It continues to meet on the third Wednesday of every month. That first meeting was rapidly followed by the first editorial attacking it for excluding the public. "Are any members of the Common Council ashamed of what they are doing that they propose to sit with closed doors," the *Independent* said.

In the year New Britain became a city, Seth J. North had been dead for 20 years. He had not been forgotten. North was a man "great of influence and power. You could never enter his presence without feeling this," wrote Peck. Andrews, who likely differed with North on abolition and church issues, closed his

507-page history with these words about North: "Being ambitious to accumulate, a combination of circumstances seemed to conspire to gratify his desire. His tact and talent for business, his wealth, his public benefactions, and private charities, have secured for him a reputation in this direction to which few ever attain." Wrote Stanley of North: "Since his death larger enterprises of a public character and more extensive business affairs have followed, the result in part of his teachings and example."

3

GENIUSES, PHILOSOPHERS, AND ROGUES

New Britain's name and manufacturing reputation spread as a result of the inscription stamped on many of its products. "Made in New Britain," was a mark of pride, especially for those who remembered the city's agrarian beginnings. But there were others in the community who made New Britain famous, for reasons good and bad. Leading them was Elihu Burritt, a person of remarkable intellectual capability and exceptional social conscience, who today remains the city's most revered historical figure.

Burritt was born in 1810, the eighth of 10 children. If he had never been born, the Burritt family would have still become famous as a result of Burritt's older brother Elijah. Elijah, born in 1794, was trained as a blacksmith and attended Williams College. A teacher, he was the author of *Logarithmic Arithmetic* and *A Geography for the Heavens: A Celestial Atlas.* The latter, a widely used textbook that was considered a standard, remained in use long after Elijah's death in 1838.

Elijah was fortunate to have attended college. But the death of his father, when Elihu was 15, cut the family off from some of its resources. Elihu, however, wanted at least to be near a college, and at 22 he moved to New Haven. He studied Greek, Hebrew, and other languages while living in a boardinghouse near Yale. For the most part he kept to himself and didn't seek out the help of anyone at Yale. After several months he returned to New Britain, working for a small manufacturing company and store and studying at night. When the financial panic of 1837 wiped out his savings, he made a fresh start and moved to Worcester,

Every city has numerous clubs and organizations, but few are as colorful as this gathering of the Spanish-American War Veterans Ladies Auxiliary. Courtesy, Local History Room of the New Britain Public Library

Massachusetts, near an active antiquarian library, in order to study languages. During the day he worked in a foundry. At one point he composed a letter in the Celto-Breton language of ancient Brittany (he was believed to be the first in the U.S. to learn that language), which he sent to the Royal Antiquarian Society in France. A few months later he received a large volume bearing the seal of the French society, his reward for a correct composition. It was during this period in Worcester that Burritt's ability with languages became known. Before he died in 1879 at age 69, he had mastered some 30 languages.

In 1838 Burritt sent a letter to a Worcester man offering to translate a German-language book for a fee. In the letter he described how, although his parents were poor and his education limited, he had studied Virgil and Cicero in their original languages, learned Greek grammar while doing blacksmith work, and made it a point to read two chapters in the Hebrew bible before breakfast. The letter was forwarded to Massachusetts Governor Edward Everett, who read it during a speech at the teacher's institute in Taunton. Everett invited him to dinner and offered, together with others, to send him to Harvard. Burritt declined. In a letter to poet H.W. Longfellow, who had also encouraged him to attend Harvard, Burritt, while

saying that he was ambitious, stressed the importance of manual labor in his life and said he wanted to stand in the ranks of the workingman—to prove that other people like himself also were capable of intellectual achievement.

During this period Burritt (although the origins of the nickname aren't certain) became known as the "learned blacksmith," for his intellectual achievements. He represented the ideal of the "self-cultured," or self-educated person, a popular notion at the time. Burritt became in demand as a lecturer. His decision not to attend Harvard may have been influenced by the realization that his early fame was based on his limited formal education.

But Burritt was no showman, no oddity of intellectual achievement. His lectures, like his studies, covered a wide range of topics, including war. Lectures he devoted to the issue of world peace served to involve him with others also interested in that goal. While in Worcester, from 1844 to the mid-1850s, Burritt started a weekly newspaper, the *Christian Citizen,* devoted to abolition, temperance, and peace. In 1858 in New Britain, he began publishing *North & South,* a weekly newspaper modeled after the earlier Worcester newspaper but which espoused his case for compensated emancipation as a solution to slavery, while writing to a

FACING PAGE, LEFT: Noted locally for his love of languages, Elihu Burritt is still well known in Europe as a
peace advocate. He was active in the peace conferences of Belgium, Germany, and France. Courtesy, Local History Room
of the New Britain Public Library

FACING PAGE, RIGHT: Born in April 1794, Elijah
Burritt (an older brother of Elihu) has unfortunately been
overshadowed by his famous younger sibling. Having attended
Williams College and graduated from Columbia, he became
an author, teacher, and highly respected astronomer. He was
only 44 years old when he died of fever on an expedition to
Texas. This miniature was presented in 1911 to the New
Britain Institute by his niece, Anna Strickland. Courtesy,
Local History Room of the New Britain Public Library

BELOW: May 10, 1910, the centennial of Elihu Burritt's
birth, was celebrated with a variety of events. Foremost was
a parade filled with symbolic floats. The Pythian Sisters
chose a classical theme, "Grecian Tableau," which portrayed
Pythias, Calanthe, and Dionysus. Courtesy, Local History
Room of the New Britain Public Library

made several trips to Europe, staying for long periods of time, and his lectures there attracted large audiences. Burritt was also active in the Peace Congress, serving as vice president of one 1848 meeting in Brussels over which Victor Hugo presided.

One of his most successful publications was called the "Olive Leaves," which comprised short essays, printed in numerous languages, that were mailed to newspapers here and abroad. Many were published. The essays often included statistics that Burritt used to illustrate the folly of war.

While Burritt's efforts for world peace through arbitration of differences rather than war ultimately were futile, one effort that he considered important for international understanding was not: his campaign for "Ocean Penny Postage." At the time it cost 25 cents to send a letter to Europe, a price that was very high for the average working person. His efforts led to international agreements in the mid-1850s to lower the price of postage.

In 1865 he was appointed consular agent for the U.S. at Birmingham, England, where he served until about 1870, when he returned to the U.S. and lived out the last 10 years of his life in New Britain. While in Birmingham he formed the International Land and Labor Agency, which sought to seek work in America for emigrants before they arrived. In 1872 Yale awarded Burritt with an honorary master of arts degree. Before he died Burritt completed some 16 books.

much smaller extent about local issues.

Burritt also served as the editor of the *Bond of Universal Brotherhood*, the organ of the League of Universal Brotherhood, an organization seeking an end to war that he founded and successfully promoted here and in Europe, gaining a membership numbering in the many thousands. Many who joined were workingmen like himself, people for whom he had appeal. Burritt

His numerous journals and diaries are at the New Britain Public Library. Burritt spent much of his adult life living outside of New Britain, but when he returned, spending the last 10 years of his life here, he remained active, building a church/mission on Cherry Street and running a small farm. The Central Connecticut State University library is named after him, and a monument to him stands in Franklin Square.

William T. Sloper, another New Britain resident, also spent much time in Europe, but his trips were mainly for recreation. Best remembered as one of the

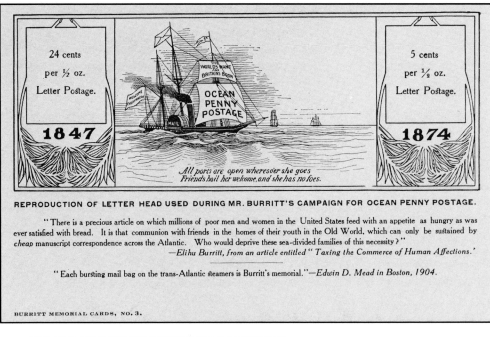

REPRODUCTION OF LETTER HEAD USED DURING MR. BURRITT'S CAMPAIGN FOR OCEAN PENNY POSTAGE.

"There is a precious article on which millions of poor men and women in the United States feed with an appetite as hungry as was ever satisfied with bread. It is that communion with friends in the homes of their youth in the Old World, which can only be sustained by cheap manuscript correspondence across the Atlantic. Who would deprive these sea-divided families of this necessity?"
—*Elihu Burritt, from an article entitled "Taxing the Commerce of Human Affections.'*

"Each bursting mail bag on the trans-Atlantic steamers is Burritt's memorial."—*Edwin D. Mead in Boston, 1904.*

BURRITT MEMORIAL CARDS, NO. 3.

Firmly believing that families and friends should be able to afford "keeping in touch," Elihu Burritt advocated the Ocean Penny postage. While abroad in 1851, Burritt visited cities in England, Scotland, and Ireland promoting his idea. At home he traveled to Washington, D.C., to address his plan to members of Congress. On October 1, 1883, four years after his death, the Penny Post was put into effect in the United States. Courtesy, Local History Room of the New Britain Public Library

---

711 survivors from the steamship *Titanic,* Sloper was more than a survivor. He was a self-made millionaire and author of *The Life and Times of Andrew Jackson Sloper,* a privately printed book of more than 400 pages purporting to tell about the life of his father, but which ended up examining the activities of some of the city's industrialists. Sloper's father, born in 1849, was an accomplished man who rose from a messenger at the former New Britain National Bank to its chief executive officer. He amassed a personal fortune and directed a number of the city's leading manufacturers. William enjoyed some of the advantages that affluence provided. The first two of the 16 long trips he took to Europe were paid for by his parents and relatives. Young Sloper followed his father into the bank in his teens, but was forced to quit after a decade in 1910 because of a physical disability (he didn't say in his book what the problem was) later corrected by a major operation. By then, however, Sloper didn't need to work. Using funds borrowed from other banks whose directors were friendly to his father, Sloper invested in local manufacturing stocks and by 1914 had made $50,000.

In 1912 Sloper, then 28, paid his own way to Europe and Egypt. Near the end of that trip, he was in the Palm Court of the Carlton Hotel in London, spending his last week overseas before returning on the ship *Mauretania,* when he came across a woman with whom he had traveled in Egypt. Alice Fortune, who was returning to the U.S. several days earlier than Sloper on the *Ti-*

tanic, convinced Sloper to travel with her. As they talked, Fortune told Sloper of an incident in Egypt. As she sat on a hotel porch, a fortune teller, wearing a maroon fez on his shaved head, passed by. Fortune asked him to read her palm. The fortune teller told her, "You are in danger every time you travel on the sea for I see you adrift on the ocean in an open boat. You will lose everything but your life." Fortune told Sloper that it was dangerous to travel with her. While the incident was disquieting, Sloper soon forgot it.

Aside from a near collision in Southampton Harbor, the early going of the *Titanic's* maiden voyage was uneventful and pleasant. The day before the ship sank, Sloper wired his father from the ship telling him the arrival date. His father received the telegram at the same moment a morning newspaper arrived with news of the sinking.

On the night of the disaster, Sloper was sitting in the ship's library writing letters when Miss Dorothy Gibson, a movie actress starring in adventure movie serials, asked Sloper if he would make it a foursome in a game of bridge with her mother and another man. Sloper joined. At the end of the game, Gibson said she was planning to take a walk around the promenade deck before going to bed. Sloper went with her. As Gibson, who had gone to her stateroom for warm clothing, arrived to meet Sloper at the head of the stairs where he had been waiting for her, the ship lurched and "seemed to keel slightly to the left." Outside they saw an iceberg. Gibson was soon joined by her mother and the other bridge player, and as they walked around the deck, they all agreed that they seemed to be heading downhill. When the designer of the ship came rushing by near where Gibson was standing, she grabbed his arm and demanded to know what had happened, but was brushed aside. Shortly after, the passengers were told to dress warmly and enter the lifeboats.

Some members of the ship's crew were telling passengers that they would be picked up as soon as it had been determined how much damage had been done to the ship. Gibson, however, thought worse and began acting hysterically. As she was entering a lifeboat she clutched Sloper's hand and demanded that he, and their other bridge partner, be allowed to get in the

LEFT: This cartoon drawn for the New Britain Herald illustrates the many facets of Andrew Jackson Sloper's career. He was active in banking, industry, church, and community affairs. He died at age 84 in 1933. Courtesy, Local History Room of the New Britain Public Library

BELOW: After the Capitol Theatre, one of the city's most popular, burned in 1942, few people would remember that it opened as Fox's Theatre in September 1913. The 1,800-seat structure housed balcony, box, and loge seats. Courtesy, Local History Room of the New Britain Public Library

of Sloper's friends and acquaintances held a party at the Farmington Country Club to celebrate his survival. In the center of the long dinner table sat a dark green painted wood tank filled with water. Floating in it were several chunks of ice and a toy ship. Sloper thought the decoration was in bad taste.

After a successful career as a stockbroker and estate manager, Sloper died in 1955 at age 71.

Sloper lived in an exciting time in New Britain, and one of the more interesting residents he knew was a fellow investor/banker, William F. Walker.

Within minutes after the Savings Bank of New Britain had opened for another day of business on Febru-

lifeboat with her. The officer in charge of loading the lifeboat allowed them to board. When the officer asked through a megaphone if there were more who wanted to get into the lifeboat, none came forward, apparently believing that the problem wasn't serious. Nineteen people plus a crew of three were lowered to the sea in a lifeboat designed for 66.

When the ship went down, wrote Sloper,

a great cry arose on the air from the surface of the calm sea where the ship had been: a cry from the throats of 1,600 people who had been thrown into the water from the decks of the ship as she went down . . . Everytime a light appeared in one of the life boats, it would be seen by hundreds of unfortunate people in the water nearby. Immediately their massed voices would rise and fall in a tremendous wailing crescendo.

Sloper wrote of the disaster as he headed for New York on the *Carpathia*. He was haunted for a time by a report in a New York City newspaper that he had disguised himself as a woman to get on a lifeboat. Sloper considered suing, but his father talked him out of it. Gibson's account of the disaster was later published and in it "she properly took credit," as Sloper put it, for saving Sloper's life.

Two weeks after he returned to New Britain, 24

ary 7, 1907, state banking examiner George F. Kendall arrived and told employees he was there to make a routine examination of the books. Thirty-year bank treasurer Walker helped Kendall count the money. But after a short while, Walker complained of a hemorrhoid problem and told the examiner he was going home to rest and would be back in the afternoon. Kendall found no problems with the cash and waited for Walker to return so that he could check the securities, which were locked in a safe whose combination only Walker knew. When Walker didn't return, Kendall left for his Suffield home perplexed but unalarmed. Walker, a baptist church deacon, treasurer of the Connecticut Baptist Society for a quarter of a century, director of the YMCA, an all-around leading citizen, had good reason for not showing Kendall the securities. Over the course of what authorities believed to have been many years, Walker had stolen $541,881 in "gilt-edged," easily negotiable railroad bonds. He also took $50,000 from the state Baptist group, nearly cleaning it out.

For the bank, which had total deposits of $7 million, the missing amount was substantial. In today's dollars, it would have totaled many millions.

The next day, after telling his wife and son that he was going to visit a New York City doctor for treatment of a kidney problem, he boarded a train wearing a long grey overcoat and black derby hat. And before he was captured in Mexico more than 10 months later, this mild-mannered thief—blue-eyed, little more than five-foot seven, 155 pounds, 63 years old—would captivate the nation, to say nothing of New Britain.

The first indication that something was amiss came several days later when Andrew Jackson Sloper, Walker's brother-in-law, received a telegram from an E.R. Merriman in New York City which said, "Mr. Walker was killed by the cars this forenoon. Letter follows." While relatives searched for Walker in New York City, bank officials took a closer look at their books. By the time

they made their startling announcement, reporters already had gotten wind of a problem. A bank run quickly developed despite assurance from bank officials that the bank's $600,000 surplus could cover any shortfall. Bank failures weren't uncommon at that time, and many of its small depositors, many of whom were Polish immigrants, crowded the bank. A Polish-speaking Catholic church pastor, The Reverend Lucyan Bojnowski, who also was a bank director, addressed the crowd and was able to end the run temporarily, but it wasn't until the bank posted notice of 90-day notification for withdrawals that the threat of failure ended.

The newspapers quickly dubbed Walker a "bank looter," "absconding treasurer," and "sanctimonious scamp." He was national news. A $5,000 reward was offered, and nearly every week brought published reports of Walker being sighted anywhere from Boston to China. The bank hired Pinkerton, a detective agency, to track him down.

As treasurer of the bank in 1862, Walker was its chief executive officer. It was a job he got through connections. Walker's first ambition was to be a newspaper editor. A printer by trade, he started a weekly newspaper in New Britain while in his early 20s. It failed quickly. Worried about the finan-

ABOVE: Little did Morton Judd know that the sapling he planted as a young boy in 1820 would grow into a local landmark. The Judd Elm stood for many years in front of his home on West Main Street. It was so large that at one point the branches extended across more than half an acre. Courtesy, Local History Room of the New Britain Public Library

FACING PAGE: The Savings Bank was built of marble and polished granite. At a cost of $100,000, this building was a veritable showplace when it opened in 1902. The interior featured quartered oak floors, mahogany furniture, and a dome illuminated by electrically lit globes. Courtesy, Herald photo files

cial security of his favorite sister, Andrew Sloper got Walker a job in 1872 as a bookkeeper in a Hartford bank. In 1879 the treasurer of the Savings Bank of New Britain, the Reverend Samuel Rockwell (who had been the first pastor of South Congregational Church) resigned because of health, and Walker got the job with Andrew Sloper's help. William Sloper, in his book, found it incredible that the bank's board of directors would consider Walker's bookkeeping experience to be ample training for a job that required making decisions about millions of dollars in investments—"subject to the approval of a Board of Directors most of whose members were nice, characteristically ineffectual, small-town dummy directors."

Walker was an intelligent man, but at a salary of $4,000 a year, he was underpaid. Walker, however, did help to build the bank's surplus and believed he was a talented investor. He told authorities after his capture that "my sole wish and desire in leaving New Britain has been to make restitution to the bank. I fled because I knew my ability as a money maker and up to

the last I have felt confident that I could repay every dollar through the mining interest I have acquired since reaching Mexico." But Walker never told authorities what he did with the money.

Police believed that Walker had been steadily losing the bank's money in Wall Street "bucket shops," where less-than-savory get-quick-rich schemes prevailed. This brought him into contact with a notorious underworld figure, Charles Gondorff, the so-called "King of the Wire Tappers." Gondorff probably found Walker desperate to make back some of the money he had lost. He engineered a "sting" operation where Walker, convinced that he had received inside information on race results through a Western Union operator, bet on false results before the real ones were posted at a bookmaking joint. Gondorff, who was never prosecuted for that crime (although he died in prison for others), claims Walker lost $85,000 through him.

Walker was captured in Ensenada, Mexico, after a U.S. consul became suspicious of him and checked his identity against a "wanted" flyer. Walker managed to fight extradition for more than six months, but on July 4, 1908, was brought to Hartford. The next day, in rainy weather, several hundred people crowded a Hartford courthouse seeking a glimpse of Walker. "They could not reconcile in their own minds that he could look the same physically as he had when he walked down Main Street daily to the bank," a *Herald* reporter wrote, "They looked for outward physical change commensurate with the change in his standing in the community following the revelations of his rascality." Walker pled guilty in a one-day trial to a number of charges and was sentenced to up to 20 years. After seven years, four months, and seven days, Walker was paroled but refused to leave the Wethersfield prison immediately because of the crowd of reporters outside. His release took place over the objections of the district attorney, who believed Walker had a bundle of cash hidden away.

He lived out his remaining years at a series of odd jobs, including a stint with an investment firm. He died of apparent heart failure in 1922 at age 78, in a bathroom of a West Main Street office building. One of his last acts was to write a letter to a French orphan girl he had "adopted" after the World War. Enclosed in the unmailed letter was one dollar.

Walker wasn't the only city person making national headlines in the early 1900s. Unlike Walker, however, the others made the kinds of headlines that made New Britain residents proud.

Ten years before Orville and Wilbur Wright made their first successful flights in 1903 at Kitty Hawk, North Carolina, Charles K. Hamilton, age eight,

took an umbrella and climbed to the roof of a barn. Imagining that the umbrella would break his fall, he jumped off. The umbrella was ruined. Hamilton was fine.

It was the first of some 60 falls Hamilton would inadvertently take from gliders, balloons, and airplanes before he died at age 27 of tuberculosis. Totaling all the falls he had taken, Hamilton figured he had fallen 10,645 feet.

Born in 1885, Hamilton was a wiry man with protruding ears, weighing not much more than 100 pounds. In his youth he earned ballooning and gliding. Accidents occurred frequently. One day, while being towed in a glider at 300 feet, the glider collapsed. Hamilton climbed into the framework of the glider while it went down in an effort to protect himself. Another time, while flying in a glider that was being pulled by a tugboat in New York harbor, another tug went under the line and cut it. Hamilton crashed into the river. It was the dead of winter. His most spectacular crash occurred on September 15, 1905, when the gasbag of a dirigible burst over New Jersey at a height of at least 5,000 feet. "The instant I heard the explosion I knew what had happened and I thought everything was over," Hamilton told a New York *World* reporter. "Down, down I went. The rush of air was so great I couldn't breathe." He survived because the remains of the gasbag formed something of a parachute which broke his descent. Hamilton crashed on the roof of a hotel. He spent three months in a hospital. The dirigible engine went through the same roof.

To those outside of aviation, Hamilton was a virtual unknown until he started flying biplanes in 1909. There was a large amount of public interest in aviation, and the flying records being set often attracted large headlines. As soon as he started flying, Hamilton started breaking records. The press reports about Hamilton soon piled up. In 1909 the Associated Press reported that Hamilton had "made a spectacular flight of 22 minutes" in Kansas City and had reached a height of 500 feet, "said to be the highest flight in America." Another AP story reported that Hamilton flew in two snowstorms and 40-mile-per-hour winds—"This is a record for daring," reported one newspaper.

As Hamilton's fame grew, his views on aviation were also reported. In one story, Hamilton accurately pre-

dicted that the perfection of the airplane would oblige the government to maintain fleets of airplanes to protect its borders, since "Smuggling will be greatly simplified." During one flight, he dropped small celluloid discs, or "peace bombs," to make a point about the military potential of flying.

In 1910, at a California airshow, Hamilton flew over the Pacific Ocean while cars raced along the coast trying to keep him in sight. He also flew to Mexico and is believed to be the first aviator to cross a national border. One of his most famous flights was a round-trip trek he made between Philadelphia and New York City. He was greeted on arrival by a large crowd that included the governor of Pennsylvania. In Nashville he made what is believed to be the first nighttime flight while a crowd of 12,000 watched. "This proves conclusively that night aviation is possible. Hereafter, airships will go day and night," said Hamilton.

While his national fame spread, Hamilton didn't forget his hometown. In July 1910 "Hamilton Day" was held in the city. An estimated 50,000 crowded Walnut Hill Park to witness an airplane flight by Hamilton. New Britain residents had been preparing for the big day for several months, and when it arrived, business in the city came to a virtual standstill. When Hamilton, after one unsuccessful effort, got the plane up, the crowd let out a large roar. Hamilton stayed in the air for five minutes. "For all time it will be written in the history of New England that the first successful flight in a heavier-than-air machine took place in New Britain, Conn., and a New Britain boy had achieved the feat. Here's to him!" an editorial in the *Herald* said.

Hamilton's one-day show was a unique event,

but New Britain frequently turned out for traveling shows, which, in the era before radio, television, and motion pictures, were major forms of entertainment. In Fairview Cemetery stands an eight-foot granite monument with a circus elephant carved on it, and a short poem underneath:

He made the hearts of children
  leap
He made both young and old
Their faith in childhood fancies
  keep
By the circus tales he told.

On the tombstone is the name of Dexter Fellows and his wife, the former Singe A. vonBreitholtz. Fellows was the chief press agent for the Ringling Brothers and Barnum and Bailey Circus. Although Fellows was born in 1871 in Fitchburg, Massachusetts, he lived in New Britain most of his life after getting married.

Fellows' start in the entertainment world came in his early 20s, when he responded to an advertisement seeking a young man to travel with the Pawnee Bill Wild West Show. Fellows had no experience with entertainment work, but he wrote a letter that impressed show officials and was hired as press agent. His job was to travel in advance of the show, post bills, and attempt to get favorable newspaper coverage. After one year with Pawnee Bill, he joined the "Buffalo Bill Wild West Show and Congress of Rough Riders of the World," working with William F. Cody, known as Buffalo Bill, and Miss Annie Oakley. But most of his 40 years were spent first with the Ringling Brothers Circus

ABOVE: "Buffalo Bill" and some members of his Wild West Show paused for this group photo with one of New Britain's finest. Courtesy, Adolf Carlson family

FACING PAGE: Connecticut's first air show took place at Walnut Hill Park in 1910, when native son Charles K. Hamilton exhibited his flying skills. Attendance was so large that more than 300 police, some from as far away as Bridgeport, were hired for security and crowd control. Courtesy, Local History Room of the New Britain Public Library

BELOW: Although the buildings are mostly gone, the church has relocated, and the park has been cut back, the memory of New Britain in the early 1900s lives on. Courtesy, Herald photo files

and then Barnum and Bailey, continuing with both when the two shows combined.

At the time of his death in 1937 at age 66, Fellows had become something of a legend—a widely known one. His funeral attracted many New Britain residents, along with a good number of celebrities, journalists, and politicians. Fellows' reputation came by way of his ability to stretch the truth, fire up the imagination, and above all, sell circus tickets.

Wearing a straw hat and a white carnation in his coat lapel and carrying a gold-tipped cane, Fellows would go to various newspapers, telling of the imminent arrival of the circus, a "scintillating kaleidoscopic, unparalleled, heterogeneous aggregation of multiplied wonders." His "dexterous adjectives"—along with an ample number of complimentary circus passes, and stories such as crossing Australia in a kangaroo pouch—usually got a newspaper's attention, a lot of publicity, and good ticket sales. In 1936 a book about his experiences with circuses was published, and in 1944 he was posthumously honored for his contribution to the circus world when a Victory ship was christened "Dexter Fellows, New Britain, Ct."

4

HEYDAY

OF THE

HARDWARE

CITY

In 1901 James Shepard, a local historian and patent solicitor, privately published a thin volume that would change the way New Britain looked at itself. Simply titled *New Britain Patents,* the book detailed every patent issued to New Britain residents and companies since the first was issued in 1810, nearly 1,450 in all. Shepard also analyzed how New Britain stood in relation to other state communities. His analysis was eye opening.

Connecticut, home of Yankee ingenuity, was leading the nation in the number of patents issued in proportion to its population—one patent to every 908 people in the decade leading up to 1900. In that same period, New Britain had one patent, on average, issued for every 367 persons. Hartford, with one patent per 511, was the closest. Shepard wrote:

Hartford is the only town that comes anywhere near us and may beat us some years but we lead in 1899 and we believe, as a rule, we are the banner town of the banner state in the banner nation and at the head of the inventive world.

The *New York Times* carried an article about Shepard's book. The headline said "A Town of Inventors," and under that, "The Record of Genius of New Britain, Conn."

The reading room of the New Britain Public Library has come full circle. Originally planned as a reading room, as seen here in 1901, it was converted into a reference area until a new addition was added in the mid-1970s. It has now reverted back to its original purpose. Courtesy, Local History Room of the New Britain Public Library

The nation's most prolific city for inventions also was a major center for U.S. hardware production. Seven of the largest manufacturers in 1903 published a book that briefly described the city's manufacturing history and closed with a diagram showing how New Britain compared with other U.S. cities in hardware production. New Britain was the largest, accounting for approximately one-sixth of the national hardware output. New Britain, they said, "is justly entitled to be called The Hardware City of America."

The industrialists had been calling New Britain "The Hardware City" some time before that book was published, but that book appeared to be an attempt to make it official. The city also was referred to, to a much lesser extent, as "The City of Toolmakers," and by as early as the late 1830s, it had gained a reputation as a producer of "nick knacks."

Until about 1850, the development of New Britain

manufacturing was limited to some extent by the money company owners could raise. That changed in 1851 when the Russell & Erwin Manufacturing Company incorporated as a stock company. The Stanley Works incorporated in the following year, and before 20 years had passed, most of those companies which would become the manufacturing giants of New Britain also had incorporated.

In 1850 approximately 300 of the town's population of 3,029 was employed in manufacturing. By the mid-1870s the number had increased to approximately 2,600, and by 1899 to 8,019. The overall population in New Britain in 1880 was 13,979, an increase of 4,449 from New Britain's incorporation as a city in 1871. In 1890 the population increased to 19,007, and from 1900 to 1920 it more than doubled from 28,202 to 59,316.

People were moving into the city because there were jobs. New Britain hardware manufacturers were expanding at a rapid rate. At the turn of the century, the State Bureau of Labor Statistics began reporting on the number of square feet of manufacturing space being added. In 1903, 279,744 square feet of new manufacturing space was built in New Britain, compared to 1.1 million square feet statewide. That was not an exceptional year. In succeeding years New Britain manufacturers added anywhere from 60,000 square feet to, in 1908, an incredible 940,000 square feet of new industrial space—an amount nearly the size of a modern shopping mall. By 1900 those manufactur-

ers were producing nearly 300 types of products, including some of the same ones the early blacksmiths had made. The major product lines were hardware, locks, and tools. Apparel was also an important manufacturing concern in the city, although to a much lesser extent.

A wide variety of items were produced in New Britain, many the result of patented inventions like the spring bed, paper box, toy pistol, electric pool table game register, washing machine, artificial leg, lawn mower, egg beater, hydraulic fire escape, mousetrap, and lemon squeezer. All but four of the inventors listed in Shepard's book are men. One woman, Alice M. Hobson, invented a steam cooker in 1891.

Of all the inventions developed by New Britain inventors, none is probably more well-known or as simple as the clothes hook. The clothes hook was a triangular-shaped wire hanger with hooks underneath to hang garments. It was invented in 1869 by Orrin A. North of New Britain and was refined by others over the decades. Today we know it as the clothes hanger.

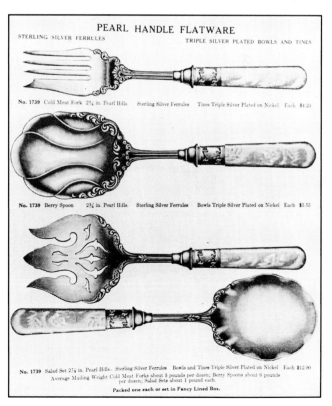

New Britain companies, especially those producing locks and doorknobs, gave much attention to the design of their products, some of which were highly ornate. In international design competitions, New Britain manufacturers won first-place awards for some of their designs, and the companies got contracts to tailor decorative hardware items for some of the most impressive buildings of the day, such as the Waldorf-Astoria in New York City.

Among the city's inventors, one of the most prominent was Justus A. Traut, who had 113 patents to his credit as of 1900—more than any New Britain inventor until then. Traut came to America in 1854 from Germany at age 14 with his father, who also was an inventor. Both father and son were hired by the Stanley Rule and Level Company. By the mid-1870s the younger Traut became a contractor, and in time fairly wealthy. Contractors were hired by companies to make products on the basis of their bid. The company would supply the tools, machinery, and raw materials, while the contractor would employ workers. Most of Traut's inventions were carpenter tools, and it was said that nearly every carpenter had some of Traut's inventions in his toolbox.

Other notable inventors included Horace Kimball Jones, a consulting engineer with the Corbin Screw Company, who had over 60 patents to his credit, including a screw machine he developed in 1879. In 1887 he started a movement for the standardization of screw threads, an effort that met with success. In 1917 Spencer H. Woods invented a machine that could detect the approach of submarines in harbors. The Navy was very interested in the device, but details on how it worked weren't revealed. By 1920 Frederick E. Carlson had received about 40 patents, the most famous of which was an eyepiece for gas masks used by the U.S. government. He also invented a gas-saving spark plug. In 1917 Nels J. Nelson designed a submarine that could remain as far as 5,000 miles from land for three months. A model of the submarine was tested in Hart's pond in Kensington. J.L. Burton Glazier, in 1913, invented a device that automatically stopped locomotives that had failed to stop when signaled. Charles W. Sevenson, assistant superintendent of the Corbin Screw Factory, invented a coaster-brake for motorcycles that was used on three-fourths of the machines then sold. By 1912 Henry G. Voight had 250 patents to his credit, most of them involving new principles and improvements for locks.

Frederick Churchill, a local attorney, wasn't an inventor, but he was a dreamer and a person very much aware of what was gradually becoming the most important development of its day—electricity. A graduate of Yale and then Harvard Law School, Churchill convinced a number of the city's leading industrialists and others to put up more than $87,000 to start an electrical development business. Most of the people who made the investment were members of the Saturday Night Club, a locally prestigious discussion group to which Churchill belonged. The foundation of the company was two Philadelphia teachers and inventors, Edwin J. Houston and Elihu Thomson, whom Churchill was able to convince to come to New Britain.

Out of Churchill's efforts the American Electric Company was formed, but within two years of its opening the company was in debt, and Churchill was unsuccessful in finding additional investors. Despondent, he committed suicide. Thomson and Houston also were unhappy. Thomson believed that the company wasn't aggressively marketing his inventions; he would eventually be awarded approximately 40 patents for electrical inventions he had developed while in New Britain. As Thomson sought out additional funding, a group of investors from Lynn, Massachusetts, approached the inventors with an offer. Out of the offer the Thomson-Houston Electric Company was formed in Lynn. The company merged with the Edison Electric Company in 1892, and from the two the General Electric Company was created.

The New Britain industrialists who originally backed the American Electric Company may have been too concerned with their own firms to channel funds into the new venture. New Britain manufacturers, which in many cases produced similar lines of products, were very competitive. And the person who may have been the best competitor among them initially didn't want to compete at all.

Philip Corbin, born in 1824, came to New Britain

at age 19, leaving his father's West Hartford farm. Corbin first went to work for Russell & Erwin, and later for North and Stanley. Within a year, he had learned enough about hardware manufacturing to become a contractor. By 1854 Corbin had become successful enough to incorporate his own company, P. & F. Corbin. At first, Corbin sought only to make products, like window springs and lamp hooks, distinct from those of other New Britain manufacturers. He considered foreign products to be his competition. The company was profitable, prompting other New Britain

manufacturers to follow suit. Corbin began venturing into the same lines they produced, like latches, bolts, and locks. He set a company policy of developing every line to its fullest extent and manufacturing goods "a little better than they need be."

Corbin, apparently, never got into the good graces of his business opponents. In the mid-1860s borough officials, connected with other businesses, won state legislative approval to establish building lines

P. & F. Corbin, the Corbin Cabinet Lock Company, and the Russell & Erwin Company merged to form the American Hardware Company, which by 1913 was the largest employer in Connecticut with 12,000 workers. Corbin died in 1910 at age 86.

Many in New Britain, through prudent investment in locally owned companies, also did well. One of the most famous of these was Darius Miller. Miller came to New Britain in 1848 to become a clerk in a dry-goods store and later opened his own store. Throughout his long life, Miller had a reputation of extreme frugality. He lived in a modest apartment above his dry-goods store, and people who knew him said the furnishings were sparse. He reused paper when wrapping packages and never threw out anything

in the borough. Their first act was to establish a 20-foot setback on a street where Corbin had planned to build a foundry. The setback made it impossible for him to build on the site. So he secretly organized a "People's Ticket" and, in a driving snowstorm on election day, was able to take control of the borough and immediately got rid of the building line. Several years later, his rivals contacted Corbin's creditors and told them, incorrectly, that Corbin's business was in danger of failing and recommended that they collect on their loans. Most of the creditors didn't. The competition hardened Corbin's management style. He referred to his company's organization in military terms and emergency meetings as "war councils." In 1902, to the surprise of many in the community with long memories,

that could possibly be reused. Miller's store was profitable, but when he died in 1919 at age 89, his estate was worth $3 million—money made largely though local stock investments. He left a large amount of money to churches and local institutions, especially New Britain General Hospital. He also left a large sum to the city, which built and named the Walnut Hill music shell after him. He left the store to three employees. When he died, his wife moved out of their apartment into a more comfortable house that they had owned, bought a limousine, and hired a chauffeur to drive it.

For those employed by New Britain manufacturers, life was often difficult. Strikes and lockouts were common, although labor violence was rare. Most strikes began over wage demands, but company efforts to break up labor organizing also prompted job actions. When strikes did occur, they often happened in several companies at once. In February 1886, for example, five strikes were reported. Stanley Works employees sought pay increases to $1.25 a day, complaining that they couldn't support their families on the $1 to $1.10 they were making. At the Russell & Erwin screw factory, the employees of two contractors struck when half their number was fired and remaining employees were told to do twice the work. In response, the company fired the contractors, took over the contracts, and rehired the employees. That action prompted other Russell & Erwin employees to strike against their contractors, and in each case the company took similar action. At P. & F. Corbin, 125 men went on strike when one employee was sent off to work in a room alone. It isn't clear from contemporary accounts why the company did that or how it was resolved. When two women workers at Landers, Frary & Clark were fired for complaining of low temperatures, other women workers walked off their jobs in protest. The two women originally fired were rehired. There are numerous mentions of women at other factories, segregated in different divisions of labor, striking and fighting exclusively male management. Women's wages, however, remained half, or less, that of men, and women often were the first to lose their jobs in business slowdowns, even though some women were self-supporting.

The city's apparel manufacturers were the largest employers of child labor in the city, and there are re-

ABOVE: Theater has always been a popular art form in New Britain. Pictured is the cast of The Belle Of New York, which played at the Russwin Lyceum in February 1914. The star, Margaret Wetmore, is seated in the center of the front row. Courtesy, Local History Room of the New Britain Public Library

FACING PAGE, TOP: Unfortunately, many young children spent their days here at American Hosiery Company while their more fortunate peers were looking forward to attending high school. Courtesy, Local History Room of the New Britain Public Library

FACING PAGE, BOTTOM: The Hawley Memorial Children's Library offered New Britain children a haven for reading and relaxing. This fireplace is still used as a site for story hours today, 58 years after it was built. Courtesy, Local History Room of the New Britain Public Library

10-percent wage increase.

The problem of child labor, despite changes in state law prohibiting it, continued for many years, prompting one truant officer to complain publicly in 1903 that parents were sending children as young as age nine off to work. But concern for children was growing, along with the need for better educational opportunities and more care for the disadvantaged. The problem was dramatically illustrated in a "child welfare exhibit," an event organized by a number of local civic groups in 1913. Attended by an estimated 28,000, the exhibit provided information to parents on how they could better take care of their children, while advocating a wide range of reforms and improved city services. Poignant photographs of New Britain children picking through garbage for food and firewood also were displayed. Infant mortality was also a major concern and an ongoing problem. For example, of the 2,844 reported deaths from 1879 to 1888, 809 were of children one year or younger, and 375 were of children aged one to five. City health officials, in a 1888 report to the Common Council, called those statistics "a sad comment on our skill in managing children." Outbreaks of infectious diseases like scarlet fever and diphtheria were frequent. In 1889 an outbreak of acute dysentery killed 52, many of whom were living in tenements in the Grove, Washington, and Beaver street areas.

Finding a place to live in New Britain could be harder than finding a job. Although there was steady housing growth (from 1884 to 1895, 654 "houses" were built, bringing the total to 2,585), newspapers frequently reported housing shortages, and existing housing was in many cases overcrowded. A large percentage of families lived with boarders, and some apartments held as many as four families living together. In the early 1900s city officials considered enforcing ordinances related to overcrowding housing, but were told by health authorities that 1,000 people would be left without a place to stay if the law was enforced.

ports of children who struck against their employers, possibly encouraged by parents who forced children into factories to supplement family incomes. In the mid-1880s one newspaper reported that "mostly children of tender age" struck at the New Britain Knitting Company seeking a wage increase. The American Hosiery Company was shut down when "20 little boys and girls" walked off their jobs seeking more pay. Some 200 other employees of that company joined them. Three weeks later, after threatening that they wouldn't reopen the company, management approved a

The school system also had trouble keeping up with the population increases, though the community worked to keep pace with the need. Until 1873 the school system continued to operate under six virtually independent school districts. In that year voters approved consolidation, and in the next 10 years they would approve construction of four schools.

The Common Council often met weekly to deal with issues of the day, including the installation of sewers, fire protection, water supply, and road and sidewalk work. One of New Britain's most enduring improvements was Walnut Hill Park, the city's first park. It originated in 1857 when a group of citizens banded together to form the Walnut Hill Park Company. They later hired the firm of Olmstead and Vaux, considered one of the best architectural firms in the country, to design the park, which comprised more than 80 acres. Later, in 1870, the park was sold to the city for the original price.

In 1857 Walnut Hill Park was pastureland on the outskirts of downtown; by 1900, however, it had been surrounded by a growing network of city streets, growing like a spider's web from the city's center. The city's factories were located

downtown on sites that, in some cases, were those of former blacksmith shops. The railway lines converged where industry was located. In the era before the automobile, many employees walked to work, and consequently most housing was constructed near downtown. By 1898, 45 miles of city streets had been constructed, mostly located within a mile of downtown's Central Park. Today there are more than 160 miles of streets. A typical factory worker's 60-hour week included an hour for lunch, which was just enough time for many to eat at home. Farming continued in New Britain at the turn of the century. One classified advertisement offered a 40-acre farm on Clinton Street, with house,

barn, and tools, for $3,500. With development came utility services. Gas service was introduced in 1855, and electrical service in 1885 when the Schuyler Electric Light Company was formed, although several of the larger factories had introduced electric lighting in their plants about five years earlier.

Social activities and community services also were organized and expanded in the city's early decades. The New Britain Institute, incorporated in 1858, charged patrons an annual fee to use its library, but in 1901 residents at a special town meeting approved a $4,000 subsidy for the library, and as a result, usage was free from then on. In 1867 the first YMCA was established, followed in 1910 by the YWCA. In 1893 New Britain General Hospital was incorporated. The hospital was originally located in the 21-room home of John and Lucy Smith at Grand and Hawkins streets. That house was first used as a hospital in 1898 when it was quickly readied to care for 34 Spanish-American War veterans suffering from typhoid fever.

As New Britain grew, so did the number of clubs, literary societies, and special-interest groups. Traveling

ABOVE: Miss McGill seems to be in firm control of her 40 fourth-grade pupils as they pose for this photo in 1907 at the East Street School. Courtesy, Local History Room of the New Britain Public Library

FACING PAGE: One of New Britain's finest assets is Walnut Hill Park, which was placed on the National Register of Historic Places in 1983. Designed by Frederick Law Olmsted, architect of New York's Central Park, this area fulfilled the dreams of the 10 men who founded the Walnut Hill Company in the 1850s. It is a haven for anyone who enjoys nature. Courtesy, Local History Room of the New Britain Public Library

theatrical performances came into town, performing at one of three theaters. New Britain also had numerous newspapers, many short-lived, to provide local news. The first such newspaper, other than the *Shepherdess* discussed earlier, was the *New Britain Advocate*, published in 1850. Other publications included the *New Britain Chronicle, The New Britain News,* and the *True Citizen,* all published prior to 1870. The *Herald* was originally

founded in 1880, but was sold in 1887 to a group, including Robert J. Vance, a former mayor and U.S. congressman, which formed the Herald Publishing Company. The Vance family purchased all the outstanding stock in 1914, and Vance's descendants continue to own the paper today. In 1902 a group of the city's industrial leaders formed the New Britain Businessmen Association, and at the group's first meeting its members discussed the city's growth. One speaker said that if New Britain were a Western city, its boomtown atmosphere wouldn't have created much surprise, "but in the old New England states, in conservative Connecticut, its record is a little short of marvelous." But the growth came with a price. Smoke from factories and trains created a serious nuisance in the city; on one occasion health authorities ordered the evacuation of respiratory patients from New Britain General Hospital because smoke was blowing in the windows.

Fire safety also was a serious problem. The potential for a devastating fire among the wood-framed buildings was always present. The city's fire department came under heavy criticism when, in 1888, fire destroyed a factory owned by North & Judd at East Main and Smalley streets, putting some 250 people out of work. "There seemed to be more officers than men,"

RIGHT: Founded in 1880, the New Britain Herald *moved to this structure in 1885. It is now the dominant daily newspaper in the area. Courtesy, Local History Room of the New Britain Public Library*

BELOW: Johnstone Vance may be best remembered as the son who carried on his parents' newspaper, but he was an adventurer at heart. An avid traveler, Vance had interests as diverse as hunting, fishing, and horticulture. Courtesy, Local History Room of the New Britain Public Library

went a report in the *Herald*, with many of the officers giving conflicting orders. The company, however, built a new factory that was one-third larger.

Taxes then, as today, were always a leading concern among voters, but the manufacturing growth and subsequent increase in the grand list were able to offset appropriation increases. For example, from 1889 to 1894, city spending (including a separate town budget before city and town consolidated in 1905) increased from approximately $67,000 to $87,500. The grand list for the same period went from $6.6 to $8.5 million. The tax rate, which was 10.25 mills in 1899, was at 10.75 mills in 1894.

The 1902 comparison of New Britain's development to Western-style growth wouldn't have been lost on New Britain residents in the 1880s. The "well-ordered" community of the 1850s was suffering from a serious crime problem 30 years later. The cause of the evil, as many saw it, was alcohol. By 1880 New Britain had 71 saloons—nearly one for every 200 residents.

More than half of the police arrests were for alcohol-related crimes, and drunkenness alone was a crime. Gambling halls were numerous and operated openly, as did prostitution. Ambrose Beatty, a three-term mayor in the 1880s, called in his 1886 annual message for greater efforts to suppress crime, citing in particular the need to abolish houses of "ill-fame." One of the most well-known of such places was called the Glaziers, on Shuttle Meadow Avenue. Despite raids initiated by Beatty and others who followed him, it continued to do business.

The movement to clean up New Britain culminated in 1893 when voters approved, 2,349 to 1,448, a measure to prohibit the sale of liquor. The state, under its "no license" law, allowed communities with referendum approval to deny saloon operators the right to operate. When the law went into effect on Halloween night of that year, saloons were packed, parties were numerous, and beer barrels were reported to be rolling in the streets. In the days immediately following, police raided those few saloons that continued to operate, and there was much chest thumping in local newspapers about the "new order" of things. "Many of the bartenders have left or will leave town today. They have obtained positions in less moral cities," commented the *Herald* shortly after the law took effect.

Although alcohol-related arrests declined, liquor continued to flow in. Once a week, it was reported, a barrel-laden wagon driven by a team of horses arrived at around 3 P.M. New "social clubs" were quickly organized, and certain private homes in the city became neighborhood alcohol distribution centers. Although the police station was filled with confiscated liquor, it

was believed that many distributors had knowledge of coming raids.

Eighteen ninety-three was the same year that the "electric train" or trolley began operating in the city. One of the first routes was to Plainville, where liquor could be bought. The train was often crowded, but liquor could be bought at many places in New Britain. Before the prohibition law was enacted, "there were 80 places where liquor was sold in the city, now there are 120. That is temperance work for you, is it not," said one local minister, The Reverend Hezekial Davis, in the *Herald.*

One year after the law was passed it was repealed by a majority of 1,168. The law died not because it was ineffective, but because many residents traveling to Plainville by trolley (or Hartford by train) to buy liquor also were doing other shopping in those towns. Local restaurants also suffered a loss of business. Liquor licenses were an important source of revenue. That revenue loss forced a tax increase. Business turndowns were frequent occurrences, but in the same year that New Britain banned liquor, it was also severely hurt by a national financial panic. Industrial production was cut back an average of 25 percent, and many employees took pay cuts as large as 20 percent. The city's Sewer Commission fired all single men, hiring married men in their place. Single

men could fend for themselves, the commission reasoned. One newly arrived German immigrant committed suicide when he couldn't find work, leaving a wife and child in his native country. Police found a letter to his family on his body: "I cannot find any work at all in spite of the great number of factories which are here. There are also a great number of people seeking work here."

Since separating from Berlin, New Britain had always operated an alms house to provide care, especially long-term care, for handicapped or elderly persons without family to help them. In 1883 the alms house and adjacent 25-acre town farm, at the Newington town line near present-day Rocky Hill Avenue, were investigated by a special town committee, whose members were clearly troubled by the small, poorly ventilated, overcrowded rooms in the alms house. They called it a disgrace. In response, residents approved funding to build a 38-room building.

Women, although excluded from positions of power, weren't docile. The Women's Christian Temperance Union, a powerful force behind the

liquor prohibition movement which formed a local chapter in 1882, also involved itself in other issues and activities—including offering sewing classes—and in 1895 successfully petitioned the Common Council to provide separate jail cells for women prisoners. In the late 1880s a chapter of the Sister Dora Society—an organization that strived to help self-supporting women—was organized.

In 1905 women organized the first day-care service for working mothers. An early reference to women's suffrage is noted in the minutes of an 1871 meeting of the New Britain Conversation Club, a men's group whose members included Elihu Burritt, and which over the course of several meetings discussed whether women should be allowed to vote. The majority appeared not to favor it. In the mid-1890s women did get the right to vote in school elections,

although initially few did. As the women's suffrage movement gained strength in later years, many New Britain women played an active role in seeking voting rights. One of their most articulate spokespersons was librarian Anna G. Rockwell, whose arguments for women's suffrage were published in a national magazine in 1912.

In 1905 New Britain consolidated the town and city, becoming the City of New Britain. While the charter was debated, it didn't face as much opposition as when the city was first formed. But some did oppose the charter, including Charles S. Andrews, referred to as the "sage of Stanley Quarter." Said Andrews at a public hearing regarding the proposal, "It has been said that there is no opposition to the new charter. There was not much opposition to those men arrested in Hartford the other day for murder and bank robbery."

5

A CITY OF

IMMIGRANTS

In 1857 Philip Diehl was born in New Britain, the son of German immiqrants. Shortly after his father had stepped off the boat in New York City, officials of the Stanley Rule and Level Company offered him a job. German immigrants had a reputation for their mechanical skills and were sought out by some manufacturers. Philip's early years in New Britain were hard:

I can never forget when my brothers and I were young, the prejudice that existed between the Irish, the native Americans and the Germans. The cry of "here come the three Dutchmen," by the other boys was cause enough for a fist fight. Even in school there was great prejudice shown against the German students. We were all put in certain sections of the schoolroom and looked upon with amazement and awe as the funny foreigners. For this reason we were very anxious to learn the English language.

Paul Leupold was another German immigrant who quickly learned how new arrivals were treated. Traveling by boat from New Jersey to Hartford shortly after he arrived in America in 1883, he and other immigrant passengers were made to stay below deck with the horses. He had paid for better.

Leupold worked in a factory and attended night school for two years to learn English. He became a citizen in 1888. It wasn't easy adjusting to American life.

"Like most other Germans, I kept with people from my own country. They understood me and made me feel at home." Leupold joined eight German clubs, with names such as the Concordia Sick & Death Benefit Society, Vater Jahn Lodge, Gerstaechker Lodge, Eintracht Lodge, German American Council and Teutonia Maenerchor. Every ethnic group had its own clubs. The rising number of immigrants prompted the long-

Sports played an important role in the social life of the city. The 1939 Fafnir baseball team was typical of a generation who played, rather than just watched. Courtesy, Local History Room of the New Britain Public Library

time Anglo-Saxon residents to form clubs of their own that excluded immigrants.

Said Leupold: "Americans couldn't understand us and generally we felt uneasy in their presence. I did have some American friends, but as a rule, I associated with German people." In time Leupold became involved in his community and was elected city auditor in 1898, a post he held for two terms. The experiences of Leupold, Diehl, and others were recorded in the late 1930s by Federal Writers' Project workers.

The Germans were the second major immigrant group to arrive in New Britain (the Irish were the first). Diehl was one of the earlier arrivals. In 1871 the first regularly held German-language services were held by the First Baptist Church. A German Baptist Church was organized in 1883. By the 1890s the Germans were well-established.

ABOVE: Some stores have signs, some have logos, but few can surpass this massive shoe held by a local cobbler. Truly a man with "sole." Courtesy, Herald *photo files*

FACING PAGE: The third generation of the First Baptist Church may have been one of the most elaborate in New Britain, but it was only used for 36 years. It was demolished in favor of a simpler building further up West Main Street. Courtesy, Local History Room of the New Britain Public Library

LEFT: Unity of the family often provided the opportunity for relatives to settle and establish themselves in this country. Seated is Carmella Passamano who emigrated to the United States in 1917 from Siracusa, Italy. She is surrounded by her daughters Josephine and Ann (seated), and a neighbor's child. Courtesy, Mary Passamano Shutra

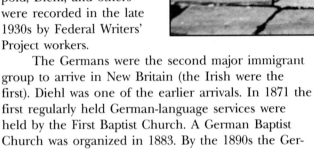

Newly arriving immigrants could expect to face discrimination and prejudice. Later immigrant groups, especially the Polish and other Eastern European settlers, would be victims of discrimination from immigrant groups that had arrived before them.

Assimilation into American society could be especially difficult for the children born of immigrant parents. As students they faced pressure from peers and teachers to Americanize, while at home their families often sought to preserve their native language and customs. One Italian child, whose parents immigrated from Sicily in 1909, was picked on in school by fellow students because of his name, Geuseppi. By the ninth grade he had had enough and got approval from his teacher to change his name to Joseph. He tried to

whitewash fences and henhouses. It appeared in six languages: German, Swedish, Italian, Polish, Yiddish, and English.

The first immigrant from Sweden to settle in New Britain was John Alfred Leonard Lundberg in 1871, but most Swedish immigrants arrived after 1880, with the largest number coming between 1890 and 1910. The first Swedish church, called the Swedish Lutheran Maria Church (later named First Lutheran Church) was organized in 1881. The first known Italian settler was Agostino Bertini in 1859. He was a well-known and popular barber. Italian immigration, however, remained small until the 1890s. The first Greek, Peter Cocores, arrived in 1897. Jewish settlers generally arrived after 1880, initially from Austria-Hungary and later from Russia. Synagogue life began in 1896 when Achenu B'nai Israel (Our Brethren Sons of Israel) was organized. It was later called Temple B'nai Israel.

It's less certain who the first Polish immigrant was. The earliest mention of a Polish name is in 1878. Polish immigrants began arriving in the city in significant numbers by the early 1880s. By 1900 there were several thousand.

The typical immigrant was a single male who would send for his family later, if he had one. Sometimes the first to arrive was an older daughter, as was the case of one young Polish woman who arrived in 1898 in New York City. After working as a domestic for a short time in that city, she came to New Britain because a distant relative was living there.

I boarded like so many others did and worked in the factory. I labored 10 hours a day and received from 50 to 75 cents a day for the work . . . It wasn't such a large pay, only when you compare it with old country roubles: it was a fortune.

She eventually married and rented an apartment. Like so many others, she took on boarders.

We had poor facilities, poor light, mostly kerosene lamps, plain furniture, of which most numerous were the beds. The men slept in one room and the women in another. There were always as many beds in one room as fitted, and at times some of the girls even had to sleep on the floor.

The hiring of foreign laborers for their skills was the exception and not the rule. Most newly arrived immigrants were hired because they would work long hours—sometimes seven days a week—for little pay. The hours made it difficult to find the time or energy to take classes to learn English. The immigrants also could be

keep the name change a secret from his family, especially his father, who wanted only Italian spoken at home. It wasn't a secret for long. "When my father learned what I had done I got the worst beating of my life," he said. But from that time on he was known to everyone outside his home as Joseph.

The immigrants came to America to escape military conscription, political turmoil, persecution, and poverty. They had heard stories, sometimes exaggerated, of the opportunities in America. The enormous gains in New Britain's population, from 13,979 in 1880 to 68,128 in 1930, was due largely to immigration. In 1910, for example, the city's total population of nearly 44,000 comprised 8,755 of native parentage, 17,037 of foreign or mixed parentage, and 18,015 foreign-born. Ten years later the city's population of 59,316 comprised 11,161 of native parentage, 26,602 of foreign or mixed parentage, and 21,230 foreign-born. At that time, this was the makeup of the city's foreign-born population: Polish, 7,804; Italian, 3,177; Swedish, 2,102; Russian, 1,152; Lithuanian, 1,246; German, 1,112; Irish, 986; and Austrian, 623. There were also immigrants in New Britain from Belgium, Canada, China, Czechoslovakia, Denmark, England, Finland, France, Greece, Holland, Hungary, Rumania, Scotland, Spain, Switzerland, Syria, Turkey, Armenia, Norway, Portugal, and elsewhere.

Communication with the substantial foreign-born population required special effort. In 1912, during a drive to make New Britain a "spotless city," a brochure was printed urging residents to plant grass and trees around their houses, remove or burn rubbish, and

used to replace any workers who threatened to strike.

Said one Polish immigrant of life around the turn of the century:

Jobs were plenty. Americans didn't care much to work for the small pay. The factories could get these new people for cheaper wages.

When someone from the old country applied for work the boss only looked down at their shoes and when he saw they were made in a foreign land he simply waved them to come and go to work.

With the arrival of each immigrant group, new clubs, businesses, churches, and cultural activities became part of New Britain. Some immigrants tended to dominate certain businesses, like the Chinese, who ran seven of the city's 12 laundries in 1908. A mission for Chinese immigrants was operated at South Church. Bound together as much by their limitations as by their shared culture, the immigrants formed neighborhoods.

The earliest city neighborhood associated with an ethnic group was called Dublin Hill, an area roughly between North, Washington, and Lawlor streets. It was here, in a time period extending to well before the Civil War, that the Irish settled. The neighborhood later became popular with Italian immigrants. The Broad Street area, which was considered the northwest section of the city around the turn of the century (when much of the area beyond it remained undeveloped), became heavily concentrated with Polish immigrants. It continues to have a strong Polish identity today.

Although there were Irish here before the Revolutionary War, Irish immigration didn't begin in earnest until around 1840. The Irish were among the first Catholics in New Britain. The first Catholic mass was held in 1842, in a private home at High and Myrtle streets. The first Catholic parish, St. Mary's, was organized in 1848. St. Mary's Parochial School, opened in 1862, was

ABOVE: In 1910 the entire city celebrated the centennial of Elihu Burritt's birth. This float honoring his peace activities was the contribution of the Swedish population. Courtesy, Local History Room of the New Britain Public Library

FACING PAGE: As general manager of the National Spring Bed Company, F.A. Porter increased the net worth of the company from $7,500 to $150,000 in only 15 years. Courtesy, Local History Room of the New Britain Public Library

BELOW: Reverend Lucyan Bojnowski (right) unified the Poles by looking after their health, welfare, finances, and education, as well as their spiritual being. Courtesy, Local History Room of the New Britain Public Library

initially staffed by lay teachers paid in part by town subsidy. Town officials saw the school as relieving some of the pressure to expand municipal facilities. But when the school, in 1878, began employing Sisters of Mercy instead of lay teachers, there was much opposition to it. The issue was raised as a ballot question and the subsidy was defeated. The first St. Mary's Church was a small structure on Myrtle near High Street. It was replaced in 1894 by a 1,600-seat brownstone, Gothic-style church on Main Street. On a rainy night in January 1902, a fire started in the basement of the imposing structure. Firefighters thought it was a minor blaze and believed they had extinguished it. They hadn't, and the church was gutted in a spectacular blaze. Hundreds of residents left their beds to watch. The church was rebuilt in 10 months and was dedicated by the Bishop of Hartford, Michael A. Tierney, a former pastor of St. Mary's.

Among the city's clergy, none would play a bigger role in the city's immigrant life than that of the Right Reverend Monsignor Lucyan Bojnowski. He was born in Poland in 1868 but was trained for the priesthood in the United States. Ordained in 1895, he was appointed in the same year as pastor of Sacred Heart Church, which had been formed one year earlier.

Before his death in 1960 at age 92, Bojnowski would be credited with creating Sacred Heart School, which opened in 1910; St. Lucien's Home of the Aged in 1925; the Daughters of Mary of the Immaculate Conception; and an orphanage, built in 1904 and later relocated to a larger structure on about 200 acres of land he had purchased in 1901 at Osgood and Corbin Avenue and Burritt Street. A Polish weekly newspaper, the *Catholic Leader,* was also started by Bojnowski in 1907. It ceased publication in the mid-1960s. For many immigrants his influence began shortly after they arrived in America because of his connection to St. Joseph's Immigrant Home in New York City, which he had purchased in 1913.

Through the institutions he created, Bojnowski sought to provide a range of services for the city's Polish population. He also exhibited considerable influence and guided many in the Polish community, to the point of being dictatorial. He was an ardent antisocial-

ist who frequently warned against it. He fought nativist attitudes, such as a 1923 proposal before the Common Council to set a curfew for children living in the fifth political ward—which encompassed the northwest section. Bojnowski's style of leadership was a source of conflict with the Polish community, and discord developed between Bojnowski and the emerging lay leadership during the mid-1920s. It was a turbulent period in which angry charges were made, and two cases of arson related to the conflict were recorded. The problems culminated in a split in the mother church and the creation of Holy Cross Church in 1927.

Blacks had lived in New Britain, initially as slaves, since the town's origins. A small black population had existed in New Britain throughout the nineteenth century. Unlike some immigrant groups, however, blacks could expect to be victims of discrimination and racism throughout their lives and down through generations. One 1887 news account reports on an attack of vandalism and theft by a band of "marauders" in a predominantly black area referred to as "nigger hill"!

One of the city's earliest recorded black residents was Lemuel Lumady, who was born in 1815 in Farmington but lived most of his 88 years in New Britain. He was employed in one of the North family's early manufacturing ventures and worked later as a whitewasher. His obituary in the *Herald* said that he "was

regarded as a pioneer resident and was treated as such."

In the early 1900s the AME (African Methodist Episcopal) Zion Church was organized. By the end of the 1930s there were an estimated 450 blacks in the city.

In addition to the immigrant waves, other events were occurring that were changing the face of New Britain. In 1907 Mayor George M. Landers won support to purchase the 1885 Russwin Hotel, described as a "white elephant," for approximately $200,000 and to turn it into City Hall. Landers, who served two terms (1906-1910), ran unopposed; he is the only mayor not to have faced opposition. Another action that would have significant impact on the character of the city was the 1919 purchase of 25 acres of land near Stanley Quarter for the Normal School. The teacher training facility needed additional land for dormitory space; commuting students were hard-pressed to find living quarters in the city's immigrant-packed neighborhoods. Work on the facility was completed in 1925. The Normal School at Hillside Place was turned over to the city school district,

which kept it until 1987 when it moved into its new head-quarters at Chestnut and Elm streets. In 1933 the Normal School became the Teachers College of Connecticut, in 1959 Central Connecticut State College, and in 1983 a university.

In 1901 the New Britain Institute Library building was erected at West Main and High streets. In 1931, as a result of a gift from Benjamin A. Hawley, the Hawley Memorial Children's Library was built. It was one of the few such libraries in the United States at the time. The Art Museum of the New Britain Institute was founded in 1903 with donations of $25,000 for the purchase of oil paintings. The paintings were hung in the institute building until the present Lexington Street facility was acquired in 1935 under the will of Grace Judd Landers. On the advice of officials of the Metropolitan Museum of Art in New York, the institute focused on collecting American art. European art was beyond the institute's budget, the officials advised. A collection of some 6,000 works has been amassed, believed to be once of the most representative collections of American art in the U.S.

City parks also expanded considerably in the first several decades of this century. The 144-acre Stanley Quarter Park was purchased in sections from 1914 to 1921. In 1928 Alix W. Stanley donated 360 acres of land, now used for a park and a municipal golf course which both bear his name. Memorials to the city's war veterans also have become prominent in New Britain. In

Central Park a Civil War memorial designed by noted architect Ernest Flagg was dedicated in 1900, and in 1928 a World War I memorial by H. Van Buren Magonigle was dedicated on top of Walnut Hill Park, once the site of a reservoir.

The First World War was an emotional period in the city. It was also one of the strangest.

On February 8, 1915, two men entered the parish house of the Lithuanian Roman Catholic Church where Father Joseph Zebris, an important figure in the Lithuanian community, and his housekeeper Eva Gilman lived. Zebris was shot four times and the housekeeper was strangled. Three months later the two men later convicted and hanged for the crime, Peter Krakas and Bernard Montvid, were captured after a running shootout in Wilmington, Delaware. Robbery was the motive, police said. But no motive would ever be found for a crime committed two years later.

It was Ash Wednesday, February 21, 1917—a day that would have an entirely different meaning for an organized group of "firebugs." Within the space of two hours, eight fires were started in a variety of downtown buildings, including the Temple B'nai Israel, then at Elm and Chestnut streets. More fires would follow, some set by time-delayed devices. Firefighters from Hartford, Waterbury, and surrounding towns were called for help. The fire damage in most cases was limited. The National Guard was ordered in. Armed citizens, with the approval of the police chief, roamed the streets for suspects. "Suspicious characters" were rounded up. When several suspects were taken to the police station, a waiting mob demanded their immediate lynching. In the days that followed, city officials feared that the firebugs intended to destroy city facto-

nades, trench knives, sabers, gun sights, and the only aircraft guns used in the United States. One thing no longer being made in New Britain was the Corbin car. Advertised as made with "New England quality," they were manufactured from 1904 to 1911. The company continued to operate a repair garage until 1939.

News of the war's end arrived by teletype in the *Herald*'s newsroom at 2:45 P.M., November 11, 1918. Industrial executives were notified, and factory whistles started blowing in the predawn hours. Thousands poured into the city's center.

Of the approximately 4,000 New Britain residents who served, 124 died—about half killed in battle or later as a result of wounds, and the others by disease or accident.

At the war's onset, Mayor George A. Quigley strongly believed that a potato shortage was possible. He had workers at the town farm increase potato production, after receiving several thousand dollars from the

ries. Guards were posted throughout the city. The incident captured wide attention, and Western Union opened up an extra wire so that people could inform relatives of their safety. No one was ever arrested in connection with the fires.

For the city's immigrant population, family ties made international conditions an issue of enormous concern. In 1915 one German immigrant, in a news account, told of having 17 relatives in the German Army and boasted of that army's invincibility. In 1917 "war zones" were established in the city, where enemy aliens were prohibited from going and in some cases from working. The names and addresses of 75 German enemy-alien residents, some of whom had been living in the city for more than two decades, were published.

When one group of 200 New Britain men left one September morning in 1917 for basic training, a crowd estimated at 30,000 turned out to bid them farewell. Stores and factories closed during the send-off. A number of local women served as nurses during the war as well.

The onset of the European conflict also saw the formation of the Chamber of Commerce in 1914. Local manufacturers produced a variety of war supplies, including machine gun parts, hand gre-

ABOVE: The students of the 1917 New Britain Grammar School class carefully hold their pose. Courtesy, Local History Room of the New Britain Public Library

FACING PAGE, TOP: Although total production during an eight-year period was less than 600 cars, the Corbin made a significant mark in automotive history. Corbins won numerous race hill climbs and economy trials. Their durability can be noted in the fact that the factory garage remained open for 27 years after production ended. Courtesy, Local History Room of the New Britain Public Library

FACING PAGE, BOTTOM: This 1944 photo depicts Landers, Frary and Clark executives examining the ten thousandth quad .50 gun mount to be manufactured in the company's war effort. Courtesy, Local History Room of the New Britain Public Library

Common Council for the project. To save storage cost he had the potatoes stored in his home basement. The potato shortage never materialized, and Quigley was stuck with a cellar full of rotting potatoes. "After it was all over and ever since, I haven't been able to look a potato in the eye," said Quigley in the *Herald*.

Although he was criticized for it, the potato incident didn't damage Quigley's popularity. On the contrary, it seemed to be the kind of thinq that served to endear him to citizens. No New Britain political figure in the first half of the twentieth century played as large a role as Quigley. He was elected to eight terms—after running for the office 19 times. He served during some of the most difficult periods in the city's history: World War I (1914-20), the Great Depression (1930-34 and 1936-38), and World War II (1942-1946).

Born in 1880, Quigley never received more than a high-school education. He started as a factory worker, later became an insurance salesman, and eventually went into construction and real estate. "I'm not a politician, I'm just a citizen interested in politics," was how he described himself.

Quigley's father was of Irish descent, and his mother was born in England. While his ancestry wasn't too different from that of previous mayors, Quigley didn't share their background.

The men who led the city in its first four decades were by and large of Anglo-Saxon descent—or "old New England stock," as the newspapers were fond of saying—and were very much part of the business establishment that had run New Britain since it was formed. Of the city's first 10 mayors, covering a period from 1871 to 1896, eight were Republicans and two were Democrats. The first Democratic mayor, Ambrose Beatty, was also the first to break the English-dominated ranks of government.

Born in 1831 in Ireland, Beatty came to New Britain in 1856 and started as a factory worker. He later became a grocer. A natural leader, Beatty was appointed by a citizen's committee made up of former Mayor Frederick T. Stanley, Mayor Samuel Waldo Hart, then the city's second mayor, and Professor David N. Camp, who would follow Hart as mayor—to head the fire department. The department was called "rotten to the core," and was doing poorly in fighting a series of arson-caused fires plaguing the city at the time of his appointment. Beatty introduced a regular training schedule, reorganized the department, and disciplined or fired miscreants. For his effort he has been called the "father of the Fire Department." He served three terms, nonconsecutively, between 1878 and 1887. The city's first immigrant mayor died in 1900.

When city residents of various ethnic groups began winning important elected positions in city government, it was sometimes viewed as the "arrival" of that ethnic group. It was a concern that extended to government jobs. In 1927 the Citizens Club of the Fifth Ward, made up of the presidents of Polish organizations with a combined membership of more than 2,000, lobbied for a promotion of a Polish police patrolman to sergeant. The police and fire ranks had been dominated by Irish. No Polish officers had served above the rank of patrolman at that time.

One immigrant who did rise in the polyglot city was Angelo M. Paonessa, a three-term mayor (1922-1926 and 1928-1930). Born in 1878, he was the eldest boy of a large family that came to America when he was 10 and arrived in New Britain in 1902. In 1911 he won a seat on the Common Council and would continue in public life for nearly three decades. While mayor he took a hard stand against the Ku Klux Klan

(which was very active in the state in the early to mid-1920s) when it announced plans in 1922 to organize in New Britain. Paonessa threatened to fire any city employee involved with the KKK. The group had an active presence in the city for the next several years. Meetings, and at least one outdoor rally, were held by the group, which in 1924 burned a cross across from Paonessa's home. Paonessa died in 1948, at 71, after a successful career as a builder and automobile dealer.

The 1920s were disturbing for many other reasons. On October 12, 1924, 18-year city police veteran James Skelly was investigating what turned out to be an attempted safecracking at the Davidson & Leventhal Store on Main Street. Inside the store he was shot and killed. One of the men involved in the shooting was captured not far from the site, and he implicated his partner, Gerald Chapman. Chapman, who had earlier been involved in a $1.5-million mail truck robbery and had escaped from prison, was considered one of the most notorious crime figures of his day. He denied his involvement with the murder until the day he was hanged in Wethersfield.

Eight employees of North & Judd were killed and 11 injured on February 4, 1926, when a foundry building roof collapsed after a heavy snow. The building roof had been altered extensively without a building permit. A total compensation of $32,089 was divided among the eight families, which also received $100 each for burial expenses.

On the lighter side, city manufacturers in 1924 sought to end the practice of Charleston dancing during working hours by threatening to fire any employee dancing on company time. The popular dance consisted of 103 steps, and much rehearsing was needed. In 1926 the first girl in the history of the high school was caught smoking. It was news then. The 2,250-seat Strand—"New Britain's wonder theater"—opened up that year. By the close of the 1920s there were five theaters in the city, four strictly for movies, and one for movies and vaudeville. The number of theater seats totaled 6,000. The city's clergy succeeded in fighting a pro-

posal allowing Sunday afternoon movies. "We feel that in the course of years it will only make for further lessening of respect for Sunday in the minds of a large number of persons, especially the young," said one clergyman before the Common Council in 1927, reported the *Herald*.

During extreme hot summer weather, it wasn't uncommon for upwards of several hundred city residents to leave their steamy tenements and sleep in city parks. During one winter an 800-foot-long toboggan slide was set up in Walnut Hill Park.

Despite ratification of the Nineteenth Amendment in 1920, giving women the right to vote, women continued to be the victims of unfair employment practices. In 1927 P. & F. Corbin, partly due to a slight downturn in employment in the city, announced that married women would be losing their jobs. "Positions should be made available for girls leaving school and for other young women whose employment is their only means of support," a company official said. It was also the year when the superintendent of schools, citing the Corbin policy which was spreading to other factories, that married teachers should be fired. The superintendent believed that married teachers couldn't devote themselves to school work. In 1932 reaction to economic conditions prompted the Common Council to ban married women who were living with their husbands from working for the city.

A notable woman in the city's history was Lena Candee Bassett. She was the first president of the Suffrage Association, the Women's Republican Club, and the New Britain League of Women Voters. In a later time she might have been a candidate for

Lena C. Bassett was New Britain's equivalent to Elizabeth Cady Stanton. She was a staunch supporter of the suffrage movement and noted for her bid for a seat in the General Assembly. Courtesy, Herald *photo files*

FACING PAGE: The mention of Cremo still brings a wistful smile to the face of many a New Britain native. The brewery closed in 1955, a casualty of the trend toward nationally distributed brands. Courtesy, Herald *photo files*

BELOW: In 1938 the New Britain High School football team traveled to Louisiana to play a Louisville, Kentucky, team in the Sugar Bowl on New Year's Eve. Earlier that year, a carful of New Britain High School fans crowded into this jalopy near the gas houses. Courtesy, Herald *photo files*

first few weeks as mayor in 1930 recuperating from pneumonia. Quigley was barely conscious when the election returns came in. His temperature was 105 degrees, and a doctor who had treated him later confided that if Quigley hadn't won the election he might well have died. He took the oath of office in bed. He would face tough years as mayor.

New Britain during the 1920s was bustling. In 1925 the city issued 1,497 building permits worth a record $7.7 million, the second highest amount for any community in the state that year. Manufacturing employment levels reached more than 16,500. By 1933 less than 11,500 were employed in manufacturing,

mayor. As it was, she was the first city woman to seek a General Assembly seat. She was the society editor of the *Herald.* She died in 1957 at age 84.

Prohibition created its share of problems in New Britain during the 1920s. Liquor was readily available, police actions to enforce the law were inconsistent, and the city's police department had problems with corruption. Prohibition also put the Cremo Brewing Company, organized around 1905, out of business. A new Cremo was started following prohibition, but it closed in 1955. By the end of the decade New Britain residents were overwhelmingly opposed to the dry law.

After a 10-year absence from the mayor's office, Quigley spent his

and only about 50 build-
ing permits were issued
that year. The city's grand
list decreased, due largely
to a drop in car
ownership. From 1930 to
1934 the grand list went
from $115 to $102 million.
In 1931 real estate prices
were reported down by
20 percent.

In his first year,
Quigley set aside $100,000
for unemployed families
and announced that for
three months of that year
every city employee would
be contributing two
percent of their salaries
for the unemployed. But
tensions grew. In March
1931, a large group of
people, led by a number
of individuals said to be
Communists, marched to
City Hall pressing
demands for $500,000 in
relief funds. A crowd of
several thousand gathered, although many were
spectators. One of the alleged Communist ringleaders
was hit in the jaw by a blackjack-carrying police officer.
Quigley could have watched the scene from his City
Hall office. Following the protest, Quigley said,
"There will be no Communists in New Britain, and if
they start anything here God help them." Five were
arrested, and one who turned out to be a city
employee was fired. Quigley later sought ordinances
from the Common Council that would give the city
power to break up streetcorner meetings of
Communists and throw people in jail who made
"seditious, disloyal statements." The police were
breaking up the street gathering anyway, and the
department came under attack on the council floor.
Some aldermen defended the right of people to
engage in free speech, while others said that all
Quigley was managing to do was making martyrs out
of people who had little support to begin with.

While Quigley, the lifelong Republican, took a
hard line on communism, he instituted relief measures
some branded as socialism. In 1931 the city began a
scrip system, where unemployed residents were paid
$6.70 in scrip and 50 cents cash for two days of work

a week. City scrip was acceptable for clothing in some local stores, and the city operated a food store for scrip
transactions. A city employee who criticized the scrip system in a published letter was fired, and city officials
made no attempt to deny the fact that the employee
was fired because of the letter.

The 1932 election attracted a five-way field for
mayor, including independent, Socialist, and Communist tickets. Quigley, who faced a severe attack for his first-
year record, won by a 2,759-vote margin. The Socialist
got 247 votes, and the Communist 110. It was a personal triumph, and in a time when Republicans were fall-
ing all over the nation, it was remarkable.

The club house at Stanley Municipal Golf Course
was built by unemployed residents in 1933, under a project proposed by Quigley. Calling for volunteers to work
one day in three weeks, the project soon had more
than 1,000 volunteers. The only compensation the city
could provide was a meal for the workers and food
baskets for their families.

Recovery gradually began after 1936. But there
was almost no population growth in the city in the
1930s. It was the first time in more than 100 years that
New Britain had failed to grow.

6

REDEVELOPMENT

When George A. Quigley returned as mayor for two more terms from 1942 to 1946, he was to govern a prosperous city. Defense contracts sent employment soaring during the war years. One company, ball-bearing manufacturer Fafnir Bearing, increased its work force from approximately 1,600 in 1942 to 5,500 by 1946. Defense workers poured into the city, and people with extra rooms were urged to rent them. Even during the postwar years, when the major companies cut back their employment, they continued to be healthy, and New Britain remained a bustling city.

When the factory whistles blew, downtown New Britain would fill with people—wishing to shop at more than 300 retail stores, go to a movie, or just walk around. The city's largest department store, Raphael's, employed nearly 300. New Britain's commercial base served not only its residents, but also those living in surrounding communities. So when state officials proposed building a "superhighway" through the city's vital downtown, it struck many people as outrageous.

Before the war ended, the state was considering construction of a major east-west expressway. The plan, referred to as the relocation of Route 6, proposed establishing a four-lane highway from the Berlin Turnpike in Newington through New Britain to Waterbury and points west. This was more than 10 years before I-84, the route that now serves that purpose, had been proposed.

In 1944 city and state officials met to discuss the proposal. City government, business, and industry leaders opposed the route for reasons embodied in a Chamber of Commerce statement, which said, in part:

But why in the name of common sense would the state highway department want to pick out the center of New Britain in which to start building a new express highway, then tear down business buildings, apartment blocks, parts of factories and ruin real estate right and left, to the disadvantage and detriment of hundreds of small property owners in this city, is beyond our imagination.

State highway officials argued that the highway would be needed to relieve traffic congestion and that any

"Rosie the Riveter" was not the only woman to do her bit in World War II. Bearings were essential to the war effort, and these women were essential to Fafnir's continued production. Courtesy, Local History Room of the New Britain Public Library

immediate economic losses would be outweighed by the long-term benefits. It was the same argument the state was presenting to all Connecticut's major cities in support of a statewide highway program. But New Britain officials would have no part of it, believing that it would destroy too much of the city's grand list. Finally, in late 1945, a somewhat perturbed State Highway Commissioner William J. Cox gave up trying to convince city officials. In a letter to the editor in the *Herald,* he said:

Very frankly, it passes my understanding why your people should wish to have the important business areas of New Britain remain inaccessible . . . Your neighboring cities of Waterbury to the west and Hartford to the east are both awake to the desirability of the expressways which you would have nothing of. The urban funds now available will therefore be spent in those cities and you need no longer fear our designs upon New Britain.

Despite Cox's apparent frustration, it would not be the last time that the state approached the city with highway plans. In the late 1940s a new highway commissioner, G. Albert Hill, approached the city again with a downtown plan similar to the previous one. Mayor John L. Sullivan said a downtown highway would turn New Britain into a "ghost town" by cutting the city in two. But unlike in 1944, city officials didn't completely dismiss the idea, and in 1950 set up an advisory committee to look at the proposal. As a result of the committee's work, the Common Council approved the hiring of Robert Moses of New York (probably the most noted highway and urban planner of his time, who had designed a road plan for Hartford two years earlier) for $25,000. In May 1951

RIGHT: On a campaign stop for democratic nominee Adlai Stevenson in 1952, President Harry Truman received a challenge from Mayor John L. Sullivan that he could not refuse. With a promise of a $1,000 campaign pledge if he would touch a piano, Truman delighted the crowd by playing the "Black Hawk Waltz" on an upright that had been pushed down the street from the hotel bar. Courtesy, Herald photo files

FACING PAGE, TOP: Stores, offices, and the railroad station together equaled the Railroad Arcade, a structure in New Britain that is still missed today. Courtesy, Local History Room of the New Britain Public Library

FACING PAGE, BOTTOM: Soldiers disembarking from the train in the early war years didn't have to go far for a meal. The Armed Forces Canteen was located in the Railroad Arcade. Courtesy, Christine Balint

BELOW: John Sullivan was New Britain's most flamboyant mayor. Aside from his lengthy political career, Sullivan was an accomplished violinist; and at one time an orchestra leader whose specialty was swing jazz. Courtesy, Herald photo files

Moses presented an alternate route running north of the state's proposal, through residential areas along Allen and Lasalle streets and Washington Park heading out toward Plainville. Business, industry, and many government leaders liked the route because it didn't affect downtown. Moses said his plan would require the demolition of 148 buildings as opposed to 349 under the state's proposal, resulting in the displacement of

243 families compared to 652. It would also cost $5 million less to build. In June 1951 the Common Council asked the state to consider it, and in late December of the same year Hill announced that the state would build Moses' route. Hill's decision inflamed the considerable opposition that had been building among those in or near the path of Moses' route, especially where it cut near the heart of the city's large and politically powerful Polish community. Shortly after the announcement, some 500 attended an opposition rally at the Haller Post. One former elected official said Sullivan "would always remain an enemy of Poles if the highway is built." The route was also opposed by Lucyan Bojnowski, pastor of Sacred Heart Church.

The public outrage prompted the Common Council, only four months away from the 1952 municipal election (elections were held in April until 1965), to reverse itself and vote to oppose the alternate route. "Come hell or high water, there will be no expressway through New Britain if I can help it," said Sullivan. But state officials weren't going to change their position. Hill said the highway would be good for the city and in 1953 began buying land in preparation. Calling it the city's "greatest fight in modern times," Sullivan sought a meeting with Hill to urge him to stop the route, but Hill refused to meet with the mayor, telling him, "The time to talk has passed, the time to do is now," reported the *Herald.* Sullivan proposed a route along the city's southern boundaries, but state officials quickly rejected it, saying it would be too expensive to build. The city filed a lawsuit to stop the highway, but even that did not stop Hill.

What stopped Hill was the 1954 election. City native Abraham Ribicoff, later U.S. senator, was elected governor that year and appointed Sullivan, a close political ally, to the office of state tax commissioner. Sullivan had lost his bid for a third term in 1954 primarily because of a citywide property reassessment—the first since 1920, and an issue that attracted 1,000 opponents in one meeting alone.

Ribicoff replaced Hill with Newman E. Argraves as highway commissioner, and a state-sponsored public hearing (as promised by Ribicoff) on the highway plan was held in March 1955 at what was then Washington Junior High School (now apartments), adjacent to the proposed alternate route. Of the more than 600 who attended, the only speaker to support the plan was a Chamber of Commerce official.

Sullivan and the highway opponents won their fight on July 23, 1956, when the state announced that the relocated Route 6 would remain in Farmington, with only a small section of it touching the city near Plainville. This is the route of I-84 today.

By then, however, there was some quiet discontent about the state's proposal. New Britain had become the only city in Connecticut bypassed by major highway routes. With a population of 80,000 and growing, there was concern about a traffic-choked future.

One year after the state dropped its plan to build a highway through New Britain, the City Plan Commission reported that the city needed an expressway. "If the city is to continue as a thriving manufacturing and business center . . . the city needs to have a first-class highway connection with other urban centers." A 1958 economic survey of the city drew a similar conclusion. Wrote the survey's author, Professor William N. Kinnard of the University of Connecticut,

Born on Star Street, Abraham Ribicoff attended local schools and was the first New Britain native to become governor of Connecticut. After serving as John F. Kennedy's secretary of Health, Education, and Welfare, he served 18 years as a United States senator. Courtesy, Herald *photo files*

One of New Britain's key strengths in the past has been its role as a retail shopping center. Its strength is ebbing, not so much from increased competition from outside as from increased difficulties of reaching stores to shop. If a major improvement of roads leading to downtown is not forthcoming in the near future, retail trade in New Britain may be expected to exhibit weaker and weaker characteristics.

Economic conditions were changing. The highway that city officials rejected in the 1940s was shaping the face of the nation in the 1950s and 1960s. The suburbs were expanding. And the first signs that New Britain might lose its industry were being largely overlooked.

Shortly after Sullivan was elected mayor in 1950, he met with the city's leading industrialists. Fafnir Bearing Company President Stanley Cooper told him (as reported in the *Herald*) that the city's manufacturers "are continually being induced to move their plants to other localities in this country . . . with tax exemptions and other concessions as lures." Manufacturing plants are easily moved, said Cooper. "It doesn't pay to take too much for granted. There must be some other factor than just fondness for a place to induce local manufacturers to remain here."

About a year after Cooper met with Sullivan, the company bought 50 acres in Newington to expand manufacturing operations there. Company officials said the city didn't have tracts of land that were suitable for its purposes, and the company's decision disturbed few since, after all, its 600,000-square-foot complex was continuing its operations here. What Fafnir (along with some other companies) wasn't doing was modernizing its existing facilities; they didn't have enough land to build one of the sprawling single-story complexes that were replacing multistory structures.

In 1954 the American Hardware Corporation

closed its iron foundry and tore down some of its buildings on Myrtle Street. Prior to the closing of its Corbin Screw divison in 1950, American Hardware had been the largest taxpayer in New Britain. It was now heading into third place. Rumors about the company's future were spreading.

A growing number of problems faced northeastern manufacturers, including aging plants, high labor costs, and transportation problems. These problems, and others, were hurting city industries.

The manufacturers, located downtown, had been boxed in by residential and commercial development. Almost no consideration had been given to future land planning. The city didn't have a full-time professional planner until the second half of the 1950s. There were few large, vacant tracts of land remaining that were suitable for industry. When New Britain and Berlin separated in 1850, the city was reduced to 13.3 square miles—making today's New Britain 157th in size among Connecticut's 169 towns and cities.

In l960, 60 percent of the city's labor force was em-

ABOVE: The campaign slogan, "Let's work together" echoed the sentiment of many New Britain residents in the 1960s. With factories gone and buildings razed, citizens looked forward to a revitalization that would begin in the 1980s. Courtesy, Herald *photo files*

BELOW: The Stanley Works and other downtown interests flank the highway which cut a path through New Britain in the 1970s. Courtesy, Herald *photo files*

ployed in manufacturing (versus 45 percent in the state). Of that 60 percent, 90 percent worked in nine large manufacturing firms. There were 24,000 manufacturing employees in 1958, 17,000 in 1965, and 9,180 in 1985. The high concentration of manufacturing employment in nine industries made New Britain very vulnerable to industry decisions.

In 1959 officials of American Hardware announced that they were studying the feasibility of consolidating their operations—located in some 40 buildings on 23 acres in the heart of downtown—under one roof, and that the company would probably move out of the city because New Britain lacked land. This announcement stunned many. The company, which had been reticent about its plans when

it closed its foundry, now revealed that it had reached this decision after a decade of study. American Hardware was more than a large taxpayer; this was the company that had played a leading role in the evolution of New Britain's reputation from "the Hardware City of America" to "the Hardware City of the World" earlier in the century. In an editorial, the *Herald* said the city "cannot afford to lose American Hardware Corp . . . to do less than our very best to keep the firm here would be a form of municipal suicide."

Bernard G. Kranowitz, Chamber of Commerce director, summed up the city's problem in a 1960 statement reported in the *Herald.*

For a long time our community has taken it for granted that these large and nationally known manufacturing companies will always stay here and grow. This past year has shown that this is no longer true because some of these companies have begun to move their base of operations out of New Britain. Old obsolete buildings and lack of sufficient land area to expand have helped bring about this situation. If this trend continues this can be disastrous for New Britain, its working people, its professional people, business firms and others.

There were other problems facing the city as well. Suburban areas were beginning to cut into the city's retail market and many factory workers would follow industries to the suburbs. By 1958 capital investment and real-estate turnover in the city's downtown had virtually halted. In 1960 the city was described as being at a "crossroads," and there was a strong belief that it could preserve its industry and retail base if it took bold and decisive action. "A blight is spreading and threatening to pierce the heart of the business district," said Mayor Joseph F. Morelli in 1958. "Stores are going out of business and for-rent signs are appearing where I don't recall ever seeing them before . . . we must do something to eradicate these things before they harm the very heart of the city." Millions of dollars available in federal redevelopment funds were seen as a key to that future.

As seen in Morelli's comments, the attitude of city officials would change in the closing years of the 1950s and opening years of the 1960s. Complacency and resistance would be re-

placed by calls for decisive action to save city industry and strengthen downtown. The direction of the city's future would be set during those years. In no other way was this change more evident then in city officials' position on the highway.

New Britain needed access to the major routes that were now bypassing the city. In July 1959 city planning consultants M.E.H. Rotival presented a plan to build State Route 72 through downtown New Britain, to intersect with I-84 in Plainville and I-291 in Newington (a highway that was later scrapped and replaced with the Central Connecticut Expressway, which remains under construction today). Their highway plan would also displace more families—more than 1,100—and take out more buildings then the state's earlier proposal for a downtown expressway. "The importance of this route can hardly be overestimated," said Rotival. "The future of New Britain as a city is at stake. The impact is tremendous, but such a highway will safeguard the economic future of the city and is, in reality, an investment which will pay handsome dividends." In January 1961 the Common Council approved the Route 72 expressway, and shortly afterward the General Assembly approved some funding for the project. The state highway bureau, which earlier had planned to build a new Route 72 that would have touched only the southwest corner of New Britain, designed a route based on the Rotival report. A public hearing was held on the state's design on August 23, 1962, and officials of the Stanley Works, North & Judd, and American Hardware spoke in favor of it along with Mayor Thomas J. Meskill (later governor). Some, however, remained wary. While the highway would improve access to the city's central business district, it would also improve access to the stronger retailing center in Hartford. Those in the working-class neighborhoods in the highway's path were bitter. "I notice on the maps not one rich person is being affected," said one man at the hearing.

Delays in construction of Route 72 became a major problem for the city. Construction was to have begun in 1965, but requests for changes in the route's design, which included building a "depressed" highway,

ABOVE: At a cost of $45,000, the first Burritt School opened in January 1871. During wartime this building, named after the "Learned Blacksmith," was used by the Ration Board. In 1961 the school, which once had an enrollment of 672 students, was razed as part of the redevelopment program. Courtesy, Local History Room of the New Britain Public Library

FACING PAGE, TOP: Look in any kitchen and you are apt to find at least one "Universal" product manufactured by Landers, Frary and Clark. These are only a few of the hundreds of items produced in New Britain. Clockwise: fruit juicer, potato ricer, horn-handled knife and fork, electric toaster, and bread maker. Photo by Allen Butte

FACING PAGE, BOTTOM: Fafnir Bearing Company was part of the once-extensive plant complex of the Corbin Screw building. Courtesy, Local History Room of the New Britain Public Library

slowed its progress, as did funding problems. In 1967, several years after the state had started buying land for the downtown route, it announced that construction wouldn't begin for six to 10 years because of cutbacks in highway funding. This delay had serious implications for both the city's redevelopment efforts and its tax base. Concerned about the $7 million already taken off the grand list due to highway land buying, Mayor Paul J. Manafort warned in 1968 of "economic disaster" if the land buying continued. Some $60 million would eventually be taken from the grand list as a result of the highway. The Common Council urged the state to move "as expeditiously" as possible to build the route. Continued opposition to the route may also have been a factor in the delay. Former Mayor Sullivan never gave up trying to stop the plan. In 1964 he again urged the General Assembly, at a hearing over the route's funding, to build the southern route—one that would "go through the kitchen of the Shuttle Meadow Country Club," the *Herald* reported.

The Route 72 "central corridor" through the city opened November 1978, known officially as the "General Thaddeus Kosciuszko Highway." The branch into Newington, which wouldn't open until July 1986, was known for many years as the "Highway to Nowhere," a name given to it by Mayor William J. McNamara. Officially it was named after Ukrainian hero Taras Shevchenko. Completion of the Newington connector was linked to the fate of I-291 (a link to I-91, the major north-south route), which was scrapped in 1979 after considerable opposition from residents in the affected towns.

Building a highway was only one aspect of the city's efforts to meet its problems. Concurrent efforts were under way to rid the city of blight and to keep industry in the city. The latter had a special urgency to it.

American Hardware sought to build a one-story manufacturing facility of some 900,000 square feet on 100 acres. In 1959, shortly after the company announced its intentions to relocate with its 2,800 employees, a proposal was offered to create an industrial park for the company in the southeastern section of the city. Today it's the successful New Britain Industrial Park.

Berlin (where the company took out an option to buy a large parcel) and other towns also courted the company. But American Hardware held back on making a final decision while the city studied a plan to rebuild the company downtown. Out of those plans came the South Central Renewal Area and downtown redevelopment plans.

In 1964 American Hardware merged with Emhart Manufacturing Company, a leading manufacturer of glass containers. After reviewing previous plans, the company said it would stay if the city could provide the property then needed in the industrial park and purchase its downtown plant. Rebuilding in the downtown area would have cost more than moving. Mayor James F. Dawson appointed a "blue ribbon" committee to study the problem, but that committee couldn't act without the approval of the Redevelopment Commission, which had its own ideas about a compensation package for Emhart. Numerous proposals were formulated. Both groups ultimately were handicapped by federal guidelines governing use of redevelopment funds. Meanwhile, Berlin approved a $1.9-million improvement package designed to entice Emhart. Months passed,

and New Britain had yet to formulate a final proposal. On October 21, 1965, the Common Council approved an offer for Emhart that included $1 million for downtown buildings (they had wanted to offer $3.8 million but the federal government set a $1-million ceiling) plus $1.5 million in moving cost, $600,000 in redevelopment cost, and other incentives. Emhart rejected it that same week. In a hand-delivered letter to Dawson, company chairman David Muirhead explained that none of the proposals made public had been given to the company as an "concrete package." Dawson was philosophical about the loss, but it came toward the end of a political campaign and his opponent, Manafort, then seeking his first term, blamed him for it. The company eventually received some $2 million in redevelopment funds for the buildings. Vacated in 1969, they burned down in the infamous "Night of Fires," of June 2, 1971. The arson-caused fire destroyed much of the Emhart complex, New Britain Lumber Yard (which was in the highway's path), and some other smaller buildings.

The city may have lost a major taxpayer, but Emhart kept the jobs nearby. This would not be the case for Landers, Frary and Clark, which produced such appliances as washing machines, irons, and electric ranges. In 1950 it employed 3,000, but in 10 years its employment rolls had shrunk by more than a third. The company's work force was divided between two facilities—one downtown, and another on Ellis Street. In 1961 the company announced that it was leaving its downtown plant for some other location. The city offered the company 50 acres near its Ellis Street facility and paid $4.3 million for the company's downtown facility, in advance of funds that would be paid for the property once it was razed for Route 72. The company gave assurances that it would stay. In May 1965 electrical appliance competitor General Electric bought the company, which had been on the verge of going out of business. Four years later to the month General Electric closed the company.

In February 1967 North & Judd Manufacturing announced that it was buying a 140-acre site in Middlefield. The company cited the lack of a suitable site for relocation within the city, as well as the highway plans affecting part of its property—although efforts were under way to design a route that would bypass the North and Judd complex.

Conglomerates purchased many of the large

FACING PAGE: The New Britain Public Library is accented with pink azaleas. Photo by Jack McConnell

Vega Society Building, New Britain, Conn.

LEFT: The Vega Benefit Society helped newly arrived Swedes settle in New Britain and held meetings in this building. Vega Hall was constructed in 1897, designed by William H. Cadwell who was noted for his use of terra cotta decorations. Courtesy, Local History Room of the New Britain Public Library

FACING PAGE, TOP: In the heart of this predominantly Polish section of New Britain stands Sacred Heart Church. A Gothic granite structure, this church was dedicated in February 1904. Although one of the spires was struck by lightning and thus shortened, this building stands tall to remind the Polish of New Britain of their heritage. Courtesy, Local History Room of the New Britain Public Library

FACING PAGE, BOTTOM: Originally the home of John and Lucy Smith, this building was converted into a hospital in 1898 to aid Spanish-American War veterans who were suffering from typhoid. It was then renovated and officially opened as the New Britain General Hospital in 1899. Courtesy, Local History Room of the New Britain Public Library

BELOW: In 1886 work began on the new railroad depot, which opened on July 1, 1887. Soundly constructed of brick and granite, the depot was, for many years, the pride of New Britain. Courtesy, Local History Room of the New Britain Public Library

The Depot, New Britain, Conn.

Bird's Eye View of New Britain, Conn.

General Hospital, New Britain, Conn.

LEFT: April 9, 1988, marked the first "Show Off New Britain Expo" held at Central Connecticut State University. More than 90 exhibitors highlighted the culture and industries of New Britain. More than 7,000 people, including representatives from New Britain's "sister cities" in Japan, Italy, and Germany, participated in the daylong activities. In addition to watching skydivers land on campus, spectators enjoyed strolling around a re-creation of the gazebo that once stood in Central Park. Courtesy, Roy Temple

FACING PAGE: Every spring for the past decade, New Britain has celebrated its multiethnic cultures with a street festival called "Main Street USA." A parade, crafts, ethnic foods and entertainment draw the citizens of New Britain together. Courtesy, Chamber of Commerce, New Britain

BELOW: New Britain is still a city of contrasts—the old mingling with the new. The new highway is surrounded by old factory buildings, an abandoned school, and three of the city's 60 churches. Photo by Allen Butte

ABOVE: Rising 90 feet above one of the highest points of Walnut Hill Park, the World War I monument dominates the central city skyline. Dedicated in 1928 and recently restored, it individually lists the 118 New Britain men who died in World War I. Photo by Allen Butte

RIGHT: An abstract sculpture graces Milesky Park. Photo by Jack McConnell

companies that were leaving, such as North & Judd, Tuttle and Bailey (which closed operations in 1984), and Fafnir Bearing, which closed its New Britain operations in 1988. The Stanley Works, the city's largest taxpayer, remains independent.

As the exodus of factories changed New Britain, a citywide scandal altered its self-image. Corruption can be found in the histories of most cities, and New Britain is no different. In the 1880s it was alleged that the city official in charge of sewer construction had his horse on the payroll. There were allegations of tip-offs of police raids during prohibition. In 1951 state police made gambling arrests in New Britain that they thought city police should be making, prompting the state police commissioner to say that he had a "lack of confidence" in the police department. But there had been nothing before like "the Probe."

This was the name given to an investigation into municipal corruption that took six years to complete. There were 29 arrests—including a police chief and two fire chiefs—and 25 convictions. The probe ended when former City Personnel Director Alfred S. Pettinelli pleaded guilty on September 29, 1983, to charges related to test fixing. Following the conviction, Chief State's Attorney Austin J. McGuigan told the *Herald*:

We . . . were silent. We, all of us, will have to live with the fact that we were silent in the face of the system that involved the corruption of hundreds of people and it will do no good to try and make Mr. Pettinelli the scapegoat.

The Probe began in 1977 when state police investigated rumors that organized crime figures were paying police to alert them to gambling raids. During the investigation a blatant attempt was made to cover up wrongdoing when a pinball machine used for gambling and confiscated by police was converted back into a legal machine while it was in the police property room. A police official was arrested who later pleaded guilty in connection with the gambling aspects of the investigation.

It was in 1978 that investigators learned about the promotion test fixing from a personnel officer. Pettinelli would later testify for the state and admit that he had fixed tests for more than 100 municipal employees during his 10 years as personnel director, which ended in 1979. The Probe resulted in the demotion, and sometimes firing, of many of those involved. Pensions for

FACING PAGE: Home plate is New Britain, Connecticut! Photo by Jack McConnell

some who had retired were reduced. It was a devastating period for the city as public servants were arrested one after the another.

Even more disturbing, investigators believe that the test fixing wasn't created by Pettinelli—he just perfected and expanded the system.

On the positive side is John T. Downey, a remarkable city resident who, while working for the CIA right out of Yale, was shot down over China and held there for 21 years before being released. He was released during a thaw in relations between the two countries, and New Britain named the street through the city's industrial park after him.

Many city residents served their country in World War II, Korea, and Vietnam. World War II claimed the lives of 243 city residents, the Korean War claimed 24 city men, and 16 died in Vietnam.

The highway, the Probe, and the loss of the major manufacturers were three of the four major developments in the city in the decades that followed World War II. The fourth was redevelopment.

In March 1961 Mayor Julius J. Kremski stood next to the old Burritt School at Main and East Main streets, holding a large sledgehammer. While some 200 watched, he took a "ceremonial swing" at the 1870 structure. It would be the first of many buildings to fall between East Main and Winter streets, and it marked the start of downtown redevelopment. It was "the beginning of the rebirth of the city," Kremski said.

Before the Redevelopment Commission ended most of its work in the mid-1970s, it had embarked on projects affecting some 170 acres of downtown land. Road systems were completely redesigned to align with the highway. Hundreds of residential and commercial structures were demolished. A 1961 master plan by Rotival included drawings of a future downtown, with modern office buildings nestled comfortably alongside smokestack industries. Such a city was possible, city officials believed.

The city hadn't been indifferent to downtown traffic improvements. One of the more notable projects began in the predawn hours of August 12, 1941. A crew of 10 hired by the city cut down four large and beloved elm trees in Central Park to allow the widening of Main Street. The man thought responsible, Mayor George J. Coyle, was out of town on vacation while the controversy raged, and the now-defunct Central Park Association filed a lawsuit to stop the widening. When Coyle returned he explained that the work had been done at night so it wouldn't interfere with traffic. The widening had been approved by the Common Council, he said. Central Park would be cut back even further in the

1960s during redevelopment. Parking also was a problem. Sullivan had the man-made Lock Shop Pond downtown (which had been created in the previous century) drained and filled in 1951, turning it into a 351-car parking lot.

Redevelopment was a time when many familiar landmarks, buildings that represented much of the city's visible legacy, were eliminated. An example was the 1855 First Church of Christ, which had moved to Corbin Avenue, and was demolished in 1964. When protests were lodged over the demolition of the Strand Theater in 1972 for a shopping mall that never materialized, the attitude of the Redevelopment Commission toward historic preservation was to tell residents to "plan early" to save buildings. The Hanna Building, or Hanna's Block on Main Street, built in 1876, was listed on the National Register of Historic

Places in 1972—the same year it was torn down to make way for East Main Street improvements. The nearby Opera House at 466 Main Street (later the Palace Theater), built in 1880, was damaged in a fire in December 1980 and was torn down two months later, ending all plans to convert it into a community theater. During some of the busiest periods of the demolition work, Mayor Manafort, a Republican, faced conflict-of-interest questions raised by Democrats because of his family and financial connections with Manafort Brothers, a company founded in 1919, which was winning many demolition contracts through competitive bids. Manafort divested himself of his financial connections to the satisfaction of federal redevelopment authorities, and although there were no allegations of wrongdoing, the issue was politically sensitive.

Redevelopment did produce Newbrite Plaza, as well as a seven-story office building at Main and Bank streets, moderate income and elderly housing, some smaller office buildings, a hotel, downtown parking garages, a new police headquarters, a courthouse, and other structures. Many of the city's retail stores, however, left or went out of business. The opening of Westfarms Mall in 1974, followed by other suburban shopping areas, contributed to the decline, along with the delays in the highway and the loss of downtown manufacturers, whose employees supplied much of the retail trade. There was a proposal in the early 1970s from Hartford developer David Chase to build over $10 million in improvements, including a small shopping mall, but the Common Council rejected a tax abatement for it. He became a major office-complex developer in Hartford.

A 15-acre site in the heart of the city—an area once known as the "jewels" because of its location—which housed parts of the former American Hardware Corporation, had the interest of two developers in 1984. Tomasso Brothers, Inc., of Farmington, a company with long business and philanthropic connections to the city, and Samuel J. Heyman of Westport, a successful developer, were both vying for a 2.78-acre parcel on a key site that each needed for parking. Heyman proposed constructing up to four 250,000-square-foot office buildings with supporting retail businesses. Tomasso Brothers had an earlier option on the contested parcel under a proposal, made in 1981, to build a 130,000-square-foot office building. The council approved the sale of that parcel and another to Tomasso, believing that Heyman had enough room to build already. Heyman dropped out, and Tomasso's building never went up. However, in a search for a new city school administration headquarters in 1985, the city selected Tomasso's proposal to construct an 88,000-square-foot building on part of the site, with one-third of it sold to the city. With a promise of a major office development on the parcels, the city sold the remaining acreage to the firm.

While delays in completion of the highway were a serious obstacle to economic recovery, New Britain's institutions were generally unhampered by them and have had a largely uninterrupted record of growth in recent decades.

What is now Central Connecticut State University was started because New Britain residents wanted to insure that their children received a good education. They also wanted to show their community pride and their hope for the city's future. The university did that, and more. Now located on an 140-acre campus, the university has 14,000 students and provides full- and part-time jobs for 1,700. It plays a major role in the city's economic, educational, and cultural life. Central is the oldest public institution of higher learning in Connecticut and the sixth oldest public university in the nation.

The New Britain Museum of American Art routinely draws thousands of visitors from throughout the U.S. and the world. It is one of the oldest museums in the country devoted exclusively to American art, and its collection is nationally recognized. The museum enjoys broad community support, as evidenced by the success of a recent fund-raising drive to expand the facility.

Leading the list of institutions that provide health care is the highly regarded New Britain General Hospital, which has become one of the largest medical facilities in central Connecticut. New Britain Memorial Hospital, a chronic-care facility, also is important to the city.

The city has a museum, called the Youth Museum, dedicated to educating children, and a strong library system that is one of the few in the state open on Sundays.

Although the city is relatively small, more than 13 percent of its land is devoted to park use, including the 27-hole Stanley Municipal Golf Course. Multimillion-dollar improvements to Willow Brook Park in the early 1980s resulted in the 10,000-seat Veterans Memorial Stadium, which has been the scene of national and international sporting events. Through the efforts of city officials, the New Britain Red Sox (a Boston AA farm team) played their first season at Beehive Field in Willow Brook Park in 1983. Attendance that season was approximately 140,000, and fans were rewarded with an Eastern League Championship.

A rich ethnic, religious, and cultural base adds a vibrancy to the city's daily life. New Britain's growing Hispanic population has also added much to the city's flavor. Community-based theater groups, a symphony, and a number of festivals celebrate the city's ethnic diversity. New Britain has numerous voluntary organizations that attempt to meet the needs of the sick, the elderly, the homeless, children, and neighborhoods through community organizing. In total, these things are evidence of a strong community spirit. The annual "Main Street U.S.A." is a celebration of that.

There are many people in the city's past who have served New Britain well, but none can surpass those police officers and firefighters who gave their lives in service to this city. Police officers are James Skelly (1924) and Sgt. William Grabeck (1951). A monument to them is at Police Headquarters on Columbus Boulevard. Firefighters listed on the memorial at the South Main Street firehouse are Michael T. Campbell (1937), Joseph P. Tynan (1941), George Parsons (1942), and Carl P. Dornfried (1980).

Although most of the industry that made New Britain "The Hardware City of the World" is now gone, it has left a rich legacy in the city's many institutions. In terms of the city's economic destiny, time will have to pass before we know for certain just what that legacy will be. It took 140 years (from the manufacture of the first sleigh bell) for the city to reach the level it achieved during World War II, when the full muscle of New Britain's powerful industries was brought into force. What occurred in the years following the war happened to many U.S. cities. They were epoch-making changes, and New Britain wasn't alone in the trauma.

But what of the city's future?

That was a question Herbert E. Fowler asked in his 1960 history of the city. At that time New Britain was entering a period of profound change. In the late 1950s and early 1960s, the city's urban planners envisioned four possible directions for New Britain, ranging from a suburban community at one end of the spectrum to an important regional center at the other. Fowler, writing about this, said, "With all these developments and redevelopments, what is the destiny of New Britain?" He didn't answer that question.

Since then, it is clear, New Britain leaders have set for the city the goal of becoming an important regional center, and in some respects—especially through development of the city's public and private institutions—the city has met that goal.

New Britain has been through the worst of those times, and through it all, something important has survived: the city's belief that it can once again reach greatness. It is important to remember that New Britain was nobody's first choice—it was created on swampland, near no body of water sufficient even to drive a water wheel. That it became the city it did was quite an accomplishment. New Britain's industrialists were always fond of remembering that this city was built in a place where none should have existed. It was a city that invented itself.

The key to any successful venture is the desire of people to make it happen. In 1984 downtown property owners organized into a self-taxing district to pay for downtown improvements. The city also was successful in having its downtown area designated as a state Enter-

The carrying of the harvest wreath from Sacred Heart Church marks the opening of one of New Britain's most popular celebrations. Dozynki, the traditional Polish Harvest Festival, has been held annually in New Britain since 1981. This event features the music, dance, and food of Polonia. Courtesy, Dozynki Committee

prise Zone, offering access to tax abatements, loans, and other incentives for revitalization. One result of these activities has been the renovation in recent years of a significant number of downtown buildings.

The city now invests in planning, which recently has resulted in the reuse of some previously vacant facilities—especially Fafnir Bearing's John Street plant, which became the home of Viking Aluminum Products, Inc., employing about 230. Two other noteworthy products included the conversion of a former shopping center into a manufacturing facility for Sealectro, Inc., which employs 250, and the reuse of Fafnir's Grove Street plant as the Enterprise Grove office complex. While the latter recently went through foreclosure, its long-term prospects are believed to be good.

Early in the city's manufacturing history, residents realized the importance of New Britain's central location, at equal distances from New York City and Boston. That has become an important selling point for the city. The expected completion of the Central Connecticut Expressway will give New Britain a direct connection to I-91 and another link with I-84. A new westbound Route 72 ramp, under construction at the time of this writing, will improve access to the city's downtown. New Britain's strong labor market, lower downtown parking cost, easy access to the city's center, and affordable housing stock also are seen as important

assets. A successful effort made in recent years to get toll-free calling to the Hartford exchange was seen as a major boost as well.

New Britain is working to capture significant office development. For a city that was a manufacturing center, this is both difficult and challenging. Most office growth that has occurred so far has resulted from internal expansion of existing office users. Economic development officials point out that such internal growth reflects national norms, but there also is a recognition that it won't be enough. The recent decision by ACMAT to buy, renovate, and relocate from East Hartford to the city's largest downtown office building (at Main and Bank streets) is seen as a positive sign of the city's ability to attract development from outside its borders. City institutions are also playing important roles in its economic future. New Britain General Hospital, combined with its affiliate, John Dempsey Medical Center in Farmington, is resulting in significant growth among businesses related to medical care. One such business is Metpath Laboratories, the largest medical laboratory in the state.

Central Connecticut State University has both the largest school of business in the state and the second largest cooperative education program in New England.

As the 1980s draw to a close, those concerned with economic development in New Britain believe that when the city's assets are taken into consideration along with its economic incentives, it becomes clear that New Britain is poised for dramatic economic growth.

On July 8, 1987, New Britain received a message that was met with pride by many city residents. A cheering crowd of 35,000 poured into downtown to hear then-President Ronald Reagan speak about the nation's economy. He talked about New Britain, calling this city "the place to be."

And when it comes to hard work, to a spirit of enterprise, to patriotism and love of freedom, to the strength that comes from faith and family, when it comes to the depth of character that builds a family, a community, and our nation, you can't be in any better place in America than right here in New Britain.

A survey of businesses in 1900 showed that people of Irish descent ran 27 grocery stores in the city. Michael P. Doherty ran one of these markets on Arch Street from 1915 to 1930. Courtesy, Dr. Robert J. Fitzsimmons

7

PARTNERS

IN PROGRESS

The emblem of the City of New Britain is a beehive. As industrious as bees, the people of New Britain work just as hard in their factories, shops, and offices.

The emblem was adopted during a time when New Britain was known as "The Hardware City of the World." Huge brick factories ringed the center of the city: The Stanley Works; the Fafnir Bearing Co.; Landers, Frary & Clark; North & Judd; the Russell & Erwin Manufacturing Co.; P. & F. Corbin; and, in the southern part of the city, the New Britain Machine Co. Some of the factories, such as Russell & Erwin and P. & F. Corbin, now part of the Emhart Corp., are still in the area in neighboring Berlin. But except for the Stanley Works and New Britain Machine, most of the original big factories are gone.

The people who worked in those plants still live in New Britain, and they still work as hard as they ever did. The inventiveness of the people of New Britain, in and out of the hardware industry, also remains evident.

The history of New Britain's businesses is replete with stories about people who invented ways to adapt to different situations, turning things to their advantage. The first dispatcher of Town & Country Yellow Cab, before the days of two-way radios, had to mentally calculate where the cabs were at all times. When he knew a cab would be passing, he would run to the corner, flag down the driver, and give

him a stack of orders.

New Britain Memorial Hospital, founded to care for those afflicted with tuberculosis, changed its emphasis to the care and rehabilitation of the severely handicapped when a cure for tuberculosis was found.

Kalman London, who had a growing law practice, left his firm to become a partner in what became one of the most successful travel agencies in Connecticut.

Paul Mangiafico was a hairdresser and owned a series of beauty salons and a school for beauticians. He was already a successful businessman, but to help a wire company that he partially owned, Mangiafico founded a coil company that now sells its electronic products worldwide.

The Russell & Erwin Manufacturing Co. and P. & F. Corbin both invented their share of different locks and are still inventing new ones. Merging as the American Hardware Co., the two firms also invented an automobile called the Corbin Car and manufactured a wide variety of marine goods that helped the United States win both world wars.

These are just a few of the many stories of New Britain's business and industries. Together with the following histories of business organizations that have chosen to support this important literary and civic project, they prove that the creators of New Britain's emblem had the right idea. It is a city of industry, hard work, and inventiveness.

FAMILY SERVICE, INC.

Today Family Service provides a full range of programs to meet the intrapsychic, interpersonal, and social needs of families and their individual members.

When Family Service, Inc., was established in 1894 it was called the New Britain Charitable Organization. Its purpose was to help clothe the city's poor and assist them in obtaining food, fuel, and shelter. Though it remains dedicated to helping others, the focus of the agency has changed due to the increased governmental concern for the poor that began during the New Deal era of President Franklin D. Roosevelt. In recent years the agency's focus has shifted to resolving the social and emotional needs of families and their individual members.

Originally the New Britain Charitable Organization had only one paid staff person, whose title was "agent," but today that person would probably be labeled "caseworker." The first annual report indicates that there were 1,072 applications for help, 103 of which came from so-called tramps. Of that 1,072, 197 people were given financial assistance at a total expense of $836.34. The 1989-1990 budget is approximately $750,000.

The first staff also included volunteers, known as "Friendly Visitors." These were women who made home visits, laboring against early maternal deaths, tuberculosis, poor sanitation, "demon rum," and frequent epidemics of "la grippe" and pneumonia.

The first professionally trained executive was Marie Zeitz. When she joined Family Service, Inc., in September 1949, there was just one other professionally trained social worker in the community.

In 1951 the agency changed its name to Family Service of New Britain and was licensed by the State of Connecticut to approve foster homes for children and to make adoption studies and placements. The Big Brother Program was launched in April 1966; Family Service began providing services to Plainville in 1958 and six years later merged with the Bristol Family Service Agency.

The agency has for many years maintained a counseling program that provides clinical services to the community. This counseling program has recently been restructured and named Lifeguides Counseling Services.

Family Service, Inc., moved from Court Street to its present location at 92 Vine Street, just outside Walnut Hill Park, about 20 years ago. The agency is a charter member of the United Way and a long-standing participant in the Child Welfare League of America and Family Service America.

In addition to its counseling and adoption programs, Family Service provides family and marital counseling services to the Hispanic community through the Hispanic Family Program. The Young Parents Program offers a pregnant adolescent and young mothers' group, and individual counseling, parenting, education, child development courses, and a school curriculum.

In addition, the Mount Pleasant Neighborhood Program provides after-school youth enrichment activities to strengthen the math and reading skills of low-income families in a local federal housing project and a Creative Parenting Program that trains and assists parents of infants, young children, and adolescents.

Including Michael Madigan, the agency's executive director since 1978, there are now 24 full- and part-time staff members.

Volunteers staffed Family Service at the turn of the century, when the agency was called the New Britain Charitable Organization. Clothing, coal, and food coupons were provided to people in need.

PRECISION SCREW PRODUCTS, INC.

Precision Screw Products, Inc., is an example of employees turning a bad situation to their own advantage. Faced with the loss of their jobs when the New Britain Machine Co. closed its Screw Products Division in 1960 following a lengthy strike, Angelo Lucco, Adrian Lammers, Louis Perschy, and Angelo Boccia set out on their own.

Putting their combined 75 years of experience in the screw machine industry to use, the four founded Precision Screw Products, Inc. They purchased two multispindle screw machines and set up shop on the ground floor of the old American Hosiery Building on Park Street. But they weren't there long. On August 1, 1966, they broke ground for a new structure at 299 John Downey Drive, one of the first of New Britain's latest wave of industrial parks. The business moved into the new plant one year later and is still located there.

With one employee the four orig-

The founders of Precision Screw Products, Inc., (from left): Angelo Lucco, Adrian Lammers, Angelo Boccia, and Louis Perschy.

inal owners manufactured screw machine parts for use in aircraft, solenoid valves, and ordinance materials. Their customers included Chapman Machine of nearby Terryville, and Peter Paul Electronics and Comet Manufacturing Co., both of New Britain. Comet, which is located next door to Precision Screw on John Downey Drive, is considered a sister company, having been founded by a vice-president of New Britain Machine's old Screw Products Division.

On July 21, 1977, however, Precision Screw was sold to Frederick Indoe and Walter Pomeroy. Indoe subsequently bought Pomeroy's share of the company in 1984 and is now its sole owner. Precision Screw still sells its products to local

The factory area of Precision Screw Products, Inc., contains 29 multispindle screw machines. Metal rods are inserted into the spindles and are cut by the machines into various parts.

companies such as Peter Paul Electronics and Comet Manufacturing, but other customers are located as far away as Indiana, Ohio, and Kentucky. In addition to screw machine parts for aircraft and solenoid valves, the firm now manufactures gas meter parts, bearings, hose fittings, marine parts, and computer parts.

While the company began with two multispindle screw machines, it now has 29. It also has a Computer Numerical Control (CNC) lathe machine and a wire Electrical Discharge Machine (EDM) with which it makes its own cutting tools. The firm also employs 25 people, and Indoe plans to double the plant's size within three years.

The company is run by Indoe and his wife, Geri, and William Flowers is in charge of engineering and manufacturing.

Indoe is a past trustee of the National Screw Machine Products Association, of which Precision Screw Products, Inc., is a member, and is a current director of its eastern group. He has traveled throughout the United States and Canada lecturing on screw machine price-quoting methods.

Of the original owners, Lucco died on October 5, 1972, and Perschy passed away on January 25, 1986.

A.H. HARRIS & SONS, INC.

A.H. Harris & Sons, Inc., had its lowly beginning in Finnegan's Alley, New Britain. The year was 1916. The alley was the home of Finnegan's Stable that supplied draft horses to many of the local Draymen, including Adams Express, American Express, and H.R. Walker Co. (Walker would be acquired by the Harris family in 1950.) Another occupant of the alley was Ed Dennison's Garage, where Art Harris, Jimmy Farrell, and other truckers kept their solid-tire, chain-drive trucks. Dennison's (later owned by Emil Charland) was a focal point of the city because it was also where the chauffeur-driven automobiles of the wealthy were stored until their owners called for them.

The alley was just off Main Street opposite East Main Street. Near neighbors were Murtha's and Hanna's Block, the Palace Theatre, Emma Porta's Fruit Store, Ye Olde Smoke Shop, The Fulton Lunch, the old Raphael's Department store, Lifshutz', and the old Elihu Burritt School, which stood on the opposite corner. The alley disappeared in the early 1960s through redevelopment. A new bank was recently

erected just north of the old alley entrance.

Art Harris' business back in those days consisted of all types of trucking. He hauled hardware, cast-iron stoves, tools, cutlery, and a thousand other items from the local factories to cities and piers in New York and New England. Furniture and fresh meat, cinders and cement for the World War I monument in Walnut Hill Park, slate and shingles, and even beer (when Prohibition was repealed) were trucked. Harris also bought a lumber carrier to haul materials to the site of the new Normal School (now Central Connecticut State University) and a huge snow loader to remove snow from the streets of Boston and New Britain. There was even a time when he attempted to compete, on an unprofessional basis, with the New Haven Railroad by operating a bus route between New Britain and Hartford.

One of the many jobs he had was hauling "clinkers" out of the boiler room of local factories. These clinkers, or cinders, made an excellent underbed for the thousands of slates that the city specified for sidewalks. Art Harris would park a Mack dump truck under a boiler room chute until the truck was full, then deliver the load to sidewalk contractors for a fee. The profit must

Arthur H. Harris, Sr., founder of A.H. Harris & Sons, Inc., started his one-man business in 1916. Today the company employs 250 people at eight sites.

have been small because the two "Bulldog Macks," after sitting for years in Finnegan's stable, were sold to the City of New York in 1935 for construction of the World's Fair.

Those were the lean years of the Great Depression and the New Deal. Factory shipments were down, and the freight business was highly competitive and unregulated. Truckers cut prices to the bone to produce income and to survive. Harris survived by delivering and unloading meat and meat products to the hundreds of small stores that dotted every street corner. The meat was hauled on small, red Ford trucks with white canvas bodies. Refrigerated trucks were unknown at that time.

The company grew, prospered, and in 1936 moved to a larger facility at 1283 East Street that it purchased from Matthew J. Hayes, Sr., a local builder. The new structure provided not only the room for the

The "Sons" of A.H. Harris & Sons, Inc. From left: Richard, Robert, Roderick, and Arthur "Archie" Jr. Roderick passed away in February 1988.

trucks but also the room to expand the line of construction products and manufacture highway expansion joints.

Harris bought the patent rights to a steel device that when poured into concrete roads kept the pavement joints level and even. This occurred in 1934, the year before the first section of the Merritt Parkway was built. The steel joints proved so successful that they were specified and used in almost every mile of concrete pavement in Connecticut for the next 30 years.

The period from 1941 to 1945 was a lean one. Construction and construction products disappeared, and the company again earned most of its revenue from unloading and trucking meat products. The postwar years changed all that.

Construction, nearly nonexistent during the Great Depression and World War II, suddenly became the nation's number-one priority. There was a rush to build houses, schools, stores, highways, and bridges. Harris' prewar experiences and reputation in the construction industry positioned the firm to become a major supplier of the needed products.

The postwar years also brought

Walker Crane & Rigging Company employees hoist concrete forms onto a flatbed truck at A.H. Harris & Sons' loading dock on Ellis Street.

about a name change for the company. Art Harris had four sons active in the business. Each had taken jobs elsewhere but had rejoined the firm. The logical name had to be A.H. Harris & Sons. It was incorporated in 1955.

Growth was rapid. The interstate highway system required hundreds of thousands of feet of the Harris highway dowel assembly and expansion joints. Concrete-forming items were needed on every structure from schools to bridges. National manufacturers asked Harris to handle their lines wherever they could be sold. With New Britain as headquarters, the firm began to establish branch locations in other states in 1959.

Currently A.H. Harris & Sons, Inc., is the largest independent distributor of construction specialties in the United States, with distribution centers in Boston, Massachusetts; Albany, New York; Portsmouth, New Hampshire; Newark, New Jersey; Buffalo, New York; and Lenoir and Greensboro, North Carolina.

The Harris Brothers Building at 321 Ellis Street. In addition to housing A.H. Harris & Sons, Inc., the former Landers, Frary & Clark factory accommodates Walker Crane & Rigging Company, another Harris family enterprise.

Today the Harris family's presence in New Britain is best seen in the Harris Building on Ellis Street. This 600,000-square-foot complex was purchased in 1970 from the General Electric Company. The building was erected by Landers, Frary and Clark, a major manufacturer in New Britain for more than 100 years and known throughout the world for its Universal trademark. Today it houses more than 60 tenants, including A.H. Harris & Sons, Inc., and Walker Crane & Rigging Company. Many of them are start-up companies that hope to own their own building some day. One such start-up company, Arthur Industries (a Harris Company), is now in its own 110,000-square-foot facility in Terryville, Connecticut.

Walker Crane & Rigging Company, Inc. (also a Harris Company) began its long history in 1883 as the H.R. Walker Co. It was located on Commercial Street next to the old police station before moving to Stanley and South streets and then to Whiting Street. It is said that H.R. Walker Co. once owned more than 100 horses and 300 horse-drawn wagons. The Harris family purchased the business from the Walker family in 1950. The Walker Crane & Rigging Company today has the cranes, trucks, equipment, and manpower to move any large or heavy objects.

PETER PAUL ELECTRONICS, CO., INC.

Career changes have become more and more common during the 1980s, but they were rare in the 1940s, particularly changes from one field to a totally unrelated one.

Paul Mangiafico took the challenge, however, beginning in 1947. Mr. Mangiafico was a hairdresser. He began as a barber in his native Italy at the age of 14, came to the United States in 1918, and was one of the original beauticians in New Britain, setting up shop over the former Raphael's Department Store at Main Street and Columbus Boulevard. The business grew, and he established a string of beauty salons and ran a hairdressing school.

Mr. Mangiafico also owned an interest in a wire mill in Winsted. In an effort to help the mill expand, he looked for a product that incorporated wire and was also needed by industry. The answer was the Peter Paul Coil Co., a firm Mr. Mangiafico founded in 1947 with Peter Yaross, another hairdresser. The product was electromagnetic coils for the radio and valve industries. Originally employing six people at

19 Walnut Street, the company also made custom coil windings.

Mr. Yaross stayed with the new venture only a few months, but Mr. Mangiafico persevered. He initially kept his hairdressing business, but steadily paid more attention to his manufacturing business. The career change was complete in 1954, when Mr. Mangiafico gave up hairdressing. "He went from curls to coils," jokes Mr. Mangiafico's widow, Josephine, the firm's secretary/treasurer.

The name was changed in 1965 to Peter Paul Electronics, Inc., to reflect an expanded product line that includes electric solenoid valves used in machinery and instrumentation. Its products are sold on every continent, according to Paul S. Mangiafico, eldest son of the founder and the company's president.

Peter Paul Electronics grew quickly. In 1950 its employee roster had doubled to 12, and the firm moved to 34 Meadow Street.

The company's reputation was enhanced in the early 1950s when it collaborated with a New Haven company to devise machinery that used 500-pound coils to test the strength of airplane components. Business increased, and in 1954 the firm moved to a 7,000-square-foot factory at 251 Whiting Street. It re-

Paul Mangiafico, founder of Peter Paul Electronics Co., Inc., ponders how his life changed since leaving his native Italy in 1918. He was a successful hairdresser with several beauty salons before founding the electronics firm in 1947.

mained there for more than 30 years. Increased production required several additions, boosting the plant's size to 28,000 square feet by 1977.

The company outgrew its headquarters again. With 100 employees, its last move was completed in the beginning of 1988. The new home at 480 John Downey Drive, formerly Van Way Webco, has 77,000 square feet of floor space. Peter Paul Electronics uses 65,000 square feet and is leasing the rest—but considering that the employee roster grew to 130 within months after the move, it's not unlikely that someday the firm will again need more space.

Mr. Mangiafico died in 1979, but Peter Paul Electronics, Co., Inc., is being carried on by his eldest son, Paul S.; his widow, Josephine; and another son, Michael, executive vice-president. Meanwhile, the children of Paul S. and Michael are waiting in the wings.

From 1954 to 1988 Peter Paul Electronics called this building at 251 Whiting Street its home. The firm moved to John Downey Drive in early 1988.

TOWN AND COUNTRY YELLOW CAB CO., INC.

In 1946, after fighting in World War II, Andrew Lemnotis returned to New Britain and opened a small restaurant called the Handy Lunch at 65 Main Street with his father, Peter Lemnotis. But Andy, as he is still called today, was restless; he worked hard at the Handy Lunch, but his heart wasn't really in the restaurant business. Noting that Andy enjoyed tinkering with cars, his father suggested that he buy the failing Town and Country Taxi Co.

Lemnotis acted on that suggestion, and in May 1949 he and his brother-in-law, Charles Zissis, bought the bankrupt cab company. They began operating with three 1949 Chevrolets, competing with the Yellow Cab Co. and the Auburn Cab Co. In later years Lemnotis bought out his competition—as well as the Berlin and the Newington cab companies—and the firm is now called the Town and Country Yellow Cab Co., Inc. The organization today has 45 vehi-

cles, including 15 certificates, eight 49-seat touring coaches, 3 mini-coaches, a number of hydraulic lift school buses for shuttling handicapped children, and vans for transporting area employees.

Zissis, who sold his share of the business to Lemnotis in 1979, continued to work in a machine shop while Lemnotis ran the firm. Their original staff consisted of John Edwards, Howard Moorcroft, Judd Staples, Donald Curtis, Andy's brother John Lemnotis, Tony Marchesi, and John Chojnicki. Another original employee, Oliver Korhonen, still works for the firm as a dispatcher.

But Lemnotis says that his right-hand man in those early days was Edwards. He was the company's first dispatcher and had a knack for knowing where a cab was at any given time. There were no two-way radios at that time, so Edwards would calculate when a cab would be passing nearby, run to the corner, stop the

cab, and give the driver four or five jobs to do.

Town and Country's original location was at the Handy Lunch restaurant, where Lemnotis continued working during the day. But the minute it closed, "I'd take off my white clothes, put on my dirty ones, and work on cars."

Since then the firm has been located at Rockwell Avenue and Webster Hill, Six Myrtle Street, and 45 Myrtle Street, where Lemnotis also operated a coffee shop. When Route 72 was constructed through downtown in 1972, the company moved to Washington and Lake streets (now Columbus Boulevard), moving again, in 1984, to its present location at 191 Arch Street.

Town and Country Yellow Cab Co., Inc., is also New Britains' Western Union office. Town and Country also serves as a parent corporation to T&C Transportation and Travel Service, its Motor Coach Division.

The taxi company has given thousands of rides during the decades, but the passengers closest to Lemnotis' heart are the handicapped children he transports to area schools. He began the service in 1953.

Town and Country Yellow Cab Co., Inc.—celebrating its 40th anniversary—began as a family business, and it still is. Since 1978 Andy has served as general manager, while his wife, Mary, is president. His son, Peter A. Lemnotis, is the vice-president. His daughters, Irene Sklavouris and Andrea Chekas, are treasurer and secretary, respectively, and his son-in-law, Peter Sklavouris, is active in coach division sales and vehicle maintenance.

One of Town and Country Yellow Cab's first taxis, a 1949 Chevrolet, parked on Lyons Street. It was one of three such Chevrolets Andrew Lemnotis bought in order to get his business started.

QUINN ASSOCIATES, INC.

Using a two-story scheme to take advantage of the site, Quinn Associates, Inc., designed the clubhouse for Norwich Municipal Golf Course, one of the oldest in the eastern United States.

The move of Quinn Associates, Inc., from Avon to the old post office at 114 West Main Street gave the architectural firm a sense of community, according to Raymond A. Giolitto, one of the company's three principals.

The actual move occurred during Memorial Day weekend 1986, but the company was being welcomed by city officials before then.

"New Britain had an absolutely wonderful reception for us," says Giolitto. "We were in Avon for eight years and never felt any community involvement. We hadn't even moved here yet and we felt a part of the community."

Originally called Quinn & Associates, the firm was founded April 1, 1973, in Bloomfield by Richard Quinn with a staff of three: Quinn, a draftsman, and a secretary. Within one and one-half years, two staff architects were hired. One of them was Daniel Weston, who later became a principal with Quinn and Giolitto.

The company's big break, however, came in 1977, when the Town of Cromwell commissioned it to convert the existing high school to a middle school, design a new high school, and renovate the Edna C. Stevens Elementary School. That allowed the staff to grow to nine, which required a move to larger quarters in Avon.

That commission from Cromwell gave the firm a foothold in the public sector. Most of its work today is done for either a federal department, such as the Navy; the State of Connecticut; or for municipalities. Among its largest projects are the $24-million school renovations for the Town of East Hampton and an $18-million correctional facility for the state at the Cheshire Correctional Center. Among its smallest was the redesign of the New Britain Police Department's radio dispatch area.

Giolitto joined Quinn & Associates in March 1979 as a staff architect, and in 1983 he, Quinn, and Weston formed the new corporation, Quinn Associates Inc.

The year 1983 also saw Patricia Quinn, Richard's wife, become secretary of the corporation and its director of marketing. That was also the year in which the principals began looking for new office space, having outgrown the Avon facility.

Management became interested in New Britain after being told that New Britain would be the next "hot spot" for office development. They looked at Enterprise Grove, the former Fafnir Bearing Grove Street plant that was being converted into first-class office space. They were about to rent there when Quinn met Robert and Peter Knauss, developers of the old post office.

Quinn Associates, Inc., rented 6,000 square feet on the condition that "we design it ourselves." The office includes a floating second floor above what had been the main mail-sorting room, lots of wood finishing, and retains the marble features of the former post office lobby. It has worked well for the firm, which now employs 24 people, and gives the staff an elegant and spacious place in which to work. "We figured this is what we do every day, and we should be comfortable," says Giolitto. "We pride ourselves on our design ability and service to all our clients."

The conference room at Quinn Associates, Inc., is in the former lobby of the old post office at 114 West Main Street. The three center windows in the background are where postal clerks waited on customers.

SPRING BROOK ICE & FUEL SERVICE

In the days before refrigeration people needed ice to keep their perishable food cold enough to last for extended periods of time. Herman E. Doerr had been exposed to the ice business, his father and his grandfather having been in the trade. Though Doerr liked the business, he didn't want to join his father, Oscar Doerr, manager of the New Britain Ice Company. He wanted his own firm. So, in 1918, after serving in the United States Army during World War I, Doerr founded the Spring Brook Ice Company.

Using a horse and wagon he began delivering ice cut from ponds owned by his family to customers in New Britain and Newington. At Ward's Pond, off Lincoln Street, adja-

mally work during the winter.

The company continued to harvest natural ice until 1942, when the icehouse burned down. Thereafter the firm began buying ice manufactured by the Southern New England Ice and Oil Company of Hartford. Spring Brook now delivers packaged ice to convenience stores, package stores, gas stations, supermarkets, and restaurants.

In the early 1930s Spring Brook diversified by entering the oil business. The firm began distributing kerosene, a product it still supplies. With the invention of the oil burner the company began selling fuel oil, making it one of the first businesses in New Britain to convert homes from coal to oil-fired furna-

Natural ice, in 260-pound blocks, was cut from Ward's Pond near the Shuttle Meadow Country Club during the 1920s and 1930s, transported via this conveyor belt, and stored in an adjacent icehouse.

1962, this time to its present location in the 10,000-square-foot old Taplin Manufacturing Company building at 19 Woodland Street. The structure was renovated and partitioned, and a refrigerated ice-storage area was added, as was an oil storage and loading facility.

Doerr died in 1979, and Groth took over the following year. He is assisted by his wife, Jean, vice-president Gregory Stafstrom, and a staff of 10. In 1989 the company completely replaced its underground oil storage to conform with the new environmental laws of the 1990s.

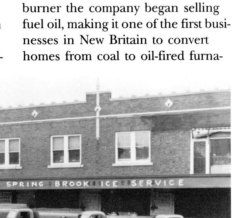

Spring Brook Ice & Fuel Service's fleet of trucks in the early 1950s. At far right is founder Herman E. Doerr. To Doerr's left is Ernest H. Groth, current owner and president.

cent to the Shuttle Meadow Country Club, Doerr built an icehouse that could hold 10,000 tons of ice. The company name was derived from the spring-fed brook that flowed into the pond.

Ernest H. Groth, Doerr's nephew and president of what is now Spring Brook Ice & Fuel Service, said it took 60 men two to four weeks to "harvest," or cut, the pond ice into 260-pound blocks. The men who cut the ice were carpenters and other tradesmen who didn't nor-

ces for central heating. At the time fuel oil was six cents per gallon.

Spring Brook was greatly affected by World War II, when the manufacture of munitions took priority over oil burners and refrigerators. Existing oil burners had to be maintained well because there were no replacements. The demand for ice also grew as war workers poured into government housing equipped with iceboxes.

In the late 1920s the firm's headquarters was moved to East Main and Spring streets and Hartford Avenue (now Martin Luther King Drive). Growing with the community, Spring Brook moved again in

Currently managing Spring Brook are (from left): Jean Groth, secretary; Gregory Stafstrom, vice-president; and Ernest Groth, president and treasurer.

FIRST CHURCH OF CHRIST, CONGREGATIONAL

The First Church of Christ, Congregational, is older than New Britain itself. It was sanctioned by the Connecticut General Court (what is now known as the General Assembly) in 1754, nearly 100 years before New Britain was incorporated. The church was a major element in the fabric of New Britain society.

According to the Reverend James Simpson, the 25th pastor of the first church to establish itself in New Britain, the philosophy of the house of worship has changed very little through the years. Simpson and the Reverend James McNair, minister of Christian education, say it is still based on the simple faith of the early Puritans. Its members are servants of each other, the community, and God. Simpson says the style of worship is simple, as are the buildings, "in form and function."

"The church hasn't changed that much in that we're still dependent upon Scripture," adds McNair. "However, we don't look at the Bible for answers as much as a

Although the church has changed buildings four times since 1754, its philosophy of simple faith, simple worship, and servitude of each other has changed little since the time of the Puritans.

guide; the words of the Bible are inspirational as opposed to literal."

Although sanctioned in 1754, it wasn't until 1758 that the church got its first minister, the Reverend John Smalley. His surname is now borne by one of New Britain's public elementary schools and by a street. He remained the church's pastor for 62 years, and was the oldest graduate of Yale University and likely the oldest New Britain resident when he died. Smalley was an accomplished theologian and scholar who taught many apprentice ministers, the most famous of whom was Oliver Ellsworth, who later became the second chief justice of the United States Supreme Court.

The original church was located near the intersection of Smalley Street and the south end of Stanley Street, adjacent to Fairview Cemetery. In fact, Fairview Cemetery was the original church cemetery.

There have been three other church locations since then. The second First Church of Christ, Congregational, was constructed in 1822 at Main and East Main streets, approximately where the Finest Super Center parking lot stands. The third church building was at what is now Bank and Main streets, where Connecticut National Bank is now located.

The fourth and final church was built in 1961 on Corbin Avenue, very near the top of Hart Street. The church and its Christian Education Wing are used by 75 groups ranging from the Prudence Crandall Shelter for Battered Women to the Orchid Growers of Connecticut. It is also used by three other churches: the New Jerusalem Bible Church, the Seventh-day Adventists, and the Universalist Unitarian Church.

"When they built this church, the idea was to go out to the world," says McNair. "It isn't just a

The third building of the First Church of Christ, Congregational, was at the present Bank and Main streets intersection, where the Connecticut National Bank is now located.

church you lock up after the Sunday services are over. It is important for churches to realize that we can't be masters of the world. We must be servants of the world."

"An estimated 2,000 people visit the church from Monday to Friday each week. There is something going on here from 8 a.m. until 10 p.m., seven days per week," says Simpson.

The biggest change in the organization of the church came in 1957, when the Congregational Church merged with the Evangelical and Reformed churches to create the United Church of Christ. Hence, the correct name is the First Church of Christ, Congregational, United Church of Christ.

SCHALLER OLDSMOBILE, INC.

The original location of Schaller Oldsmobile was on Hartford Road not far from the present intersection of Stanley and North streets. The sign in the showroom notes that the new location would be on Stanley Street, which is still the present location of the dealership; however, this section on Stanley Street has been renamed Veterans Drive.

Schaller Oldsmobile, Inc., was founded in New Britain in the spring of 1953 by Gustave Schaller as a small, family-owned dealership to serve the automotive needs of a growing community. The first year in business the company sold approximately 200 new and used vehicles.

In 1955 Schaller moved his auto dealership to Stanley Street, to the part later renamed Veterans Drive. Schaller Oldsmobile is still headquartered there. Gustave Schaller retired from the business in the early 1960s.

Schaller Auto World is now owned and operated by two of Gustave's sons, Arthur and Ronald Schaller. The company has grown to include more than 150 employees with annual sales of more than 4,000 new and used vehicles. In addition to selling Oldsmobiles, the firm also sells Hondas, Acuras, and Subarus.

The first attempt to expand beyond the Oldsmobile line of automobiles was in 1974. The company began selling a car called Bricklin,

a gull-winged sports car. But the line never caught on, and Schaller stopped selling it within a year.

Then, in 1975, Schaller took on a Renault franchise and located it across the street from Oldsmobile. Seeing no future in Renault, he replaced it in 1976 with a Honda franchise, and the company's business grew significantly.

In the spring of 1982, a new 20,000-square-foot building was con-

structed not far from Schaller Oldsmobile to serve Honda sales and service. A few months later the firm began selling Subarus. In 1985 a similar 20,000-square-foot building was constructed for the Subaru franchise.

In 1986 Art and Ron Schaller founded Schaller Acura of Manchester. Because of a Honda 10-mile run, the Acura dealership could not be located in New Britain.

In between acquiring new dealerships, Schaller also founded a car-leasing and rental division. In addition, the firm has begun an extensive auto parts wholesaling business throughout Connecticut and began construction on a new, ultramodern 14,000-square-foot body shop.

This aerial view of the 12-acre Schaller Auto World complex includes the Oldsmobile, Subaru, and Honda dealerships (each in separate buildings); the auto leasing agency and rental agency; the new and used car preparation building; and the new wholesale auto parts distribution center.

EMHART CORPORATION, HARDWARE DIVISION

The men whose names are synonymous with the early days of what is now the Emhart Corporation's Hardware Division are also part of New Britain's history. Russell is remembered in Russell Street; Erwin, in Erwin Place; Corbin, in Corbin Avenue; Stanley, in Stanley Street; North, in North Street; and Talcott, in Talcott Street.

The name "Emhart" is a relatively new one for the Hardware Division. It has had the name for 25 years, a long time for some, but not for a firm with origins dating back 150 years to 1839 and, in a way, even longer. The company evolved over the years, beginning in 1839 with the Russell & Erwin Manufacturing Company. A competing firm, P&F Corbin, was established in 1849. Then came the Corbin Cabinet Lock Co. in 1882. In 1902 the competitors merged to form the American Hardware Corporation, which became Emhart's Hardware Division through another merger in 1964.

The products the founding companies made, and the Hardware Division still makes, were builders' hardware, particularly a wide variety of locks. But the companies have also produced ox balls, gas mask filters, hand grenades, and even a line of automobiles.

RUSSELL & ERWIN MANUFACTURING COMPANY

As the population increased in the early 1800s so did the need for manufactured goods. Because iron was very accessible to the New Britain area via the Hudson River-Long Island Sound-Connecticut River water route, small manufacturing firms began springing up, producing door latches, bolts, hasps, and hinges.

Among these firms was one that had some initial difficulty keeping partners, but that did not take long

Henry E. Russell (left) and Cornelius B. Erwin (right) joined forces on New Year's Day, 1839, to lay the foundation of the Russell & Erwin Manufacturing Company. They ran the company for 46 years and were chiefly responsible for its tremendous growth during the nineteenth century.

to become a giant of the Industrial Revolution. The company, created January 1, 1839, consisted of a partnership between Henry E. Russell, Cornelius B. Erwin, and Frederick T. Stanley. It picked up where another firm, composed of F.T. Stanley, W.B. Stanley, Emanual Russell, Truman Woodruff, and Norman Woodruff, left off. They had organized four years previously and constructed a brick factory, the New Britain Lock Factory, for the manufacture of plate locks. But all except Frederick T. Stanley withdrew from the partnership in 1838, leaving him to create a new one with Russell and Erwin.

The new company was named Stanley, Russell & Co., but a year later Stanley withdrew from the organization. Smith Matteson and John H. Bowen then joined the partnership, and the name was changed to Matteson, Russell & Co. But Matteson died in 1842, and his capital was withdrawn, while Bowen ceased his relationship with the organization soon afterward. That left Russell and Erwin as the sole owners, providing a consistent policy that enabled the business to grow and prosper.

The firm's name was formally changed to Russell & Erwin in 1846.

Portrayed in this illustration are the early plants housing Corbin Cabinet Lock (top), Russwin (center), and Corbin (bottom).

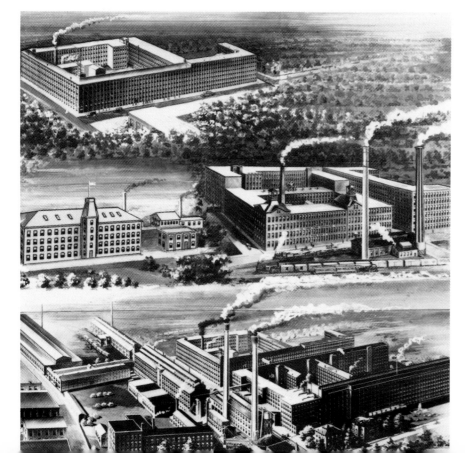

It grew four years later with the purchase of several other hardware businesses in New Britain to become the Russell & Erwin Manufacturing Company, a joint stock corporation with $125,000 in capital, in 1851.

When Russell & Erwin began in 1839, its products were sold through New York commission houses. But Henry E. Russell soon moved to New York to open a warehouse, essentially becoming the sales manager.

After the firm became incorporated in 1851, Russell served as treasurer while Erwin was president. Henry E. Russell retired in 1880, selling his estate in New Britain to his nephew, also named Henry Russell, who had joined the firm at the age of 30 in 1869. Erwin's health was failing, and he turned most of the responsibility for running the business to the so-called Henry Russell, "Jr.," but when Erwin died in 1885, Henry Russell, "Sr.," came out of retirement and assumed the presidency of the firm.

In 1849 the Russell & Erwin products catalog had 22 pages, but by 1865 it had grown to 432 pages. It sold for 25 cents per copy and included hardware, houseware, farm supplies, bells, rim knob locks, escutcheons, bear traps, and coffin handles. At that time the firm began selling overseas, publishing a 445-page catalog in Spanish in 1861. Following the Civil War Russell & Erwin's doorknobs and escutcheon plates became more ornate. In 1875 the firm added wood screws to its product line.

But builders' hardware was not the only thing Russell & Erwin produced. During World War I the firm—then a part of American Hardware—kept magazines for Browning machine guns, Sutton fuse heads for mortars, and gas mask filters flowing to the war front. The company also added marine products, equipping the fleet

with various kinds of joiner hardware. During World War II the firm played a major role in helping to destroy the Nazi U-Boat fleet by manufacturing torpedo immersion-control mechanisms and other torpedo, mine, and depth-charge components.

P&F CORBIN

Founded in 1849, 10 years after the Russell & Erwin Manufacturing Company, P&F Corbin took its name from Philip and Frank Corbin, lock contractors. Together with Edward Doen, a brass founder, the Corbins established a partnership called Doen, Corbin & Co. The three partners each contributed $300 to begin the venture. A building costing $600 was constructed on Whiting Street for the new business. It included a horsepower treadmill, a grindstone, an emery wheel, two lathes, and two furnaces for casting.

Doen stayed with the firm only a few months, and in 1851 the name was changed to P&F Corbin. The company, which was incorporated in 1854, grew beyond the capacity of the factory to produce or the partners to finance. It was decided to sell stock in order to acquire more capital. The original incorporators were Philip, Frank, Waldo, and William Corbin; Frederick H. North; Oliver Stanley; and John B. Talcott. Frank Corbin resigned as the corporations' first treasurer in 1860 to enter a separate business.

Although P&F Corbin and Russell & Erwin competed later, P&F Corbin's original intent was to avoid domestic competition. Its initial products were of a type that had been imported from overseas. The locks were equally good or better than those imported from other countries, but P&F Cor-

Railway car hardware was big business for Emhart in the late 1870s.

bin sold them for no more than the price of the foreign locks. "Something a little better than the other fellow's for the same money" is how Philip Corbin described his company's products.

P&F Corbin became famous worldwide for its locks, but the first goods the company produced in 1849 were ox balls. Doen, Philip, and Frank Corbin realized that they had to give their new company a big boost. Ox balls—rounded metal tips for the horns of cattle—were in big demand, so the three designed

An ornate order acknowledgement form used by P & F Corbin in New Britain, 1902.

Some of the first wrought steel cases for mortise and rim locks were produced by Russwin and Corbin in the 1890s.

a new pattern, improving on previous designs. The first customer was a hardware merchant from Ohio who was visiting a friend in Farmington.

P&F Corbin was among the first manufacturers to make lifting handles with bails to pull drawers open. By 1852 its product line had also grown to include flush, neck, and barrel bolts, and window springs. Wrought-brass butts, a type of door hinge, were added to the product line in 1852. They were described in the catalog as "Warranted Stronger than Cast, and true in the Joints."

The only other American firm that made wrought-brass butts at the time was the Scovill Manufacturing Co. in Waterbury. As the story goes, in order to create a preference for the P&F Corbin brass butts, the firm sold them below what Scovill charged. J.M.L. Scovill, the founder and manager of the Waterbury firm, sent an ultimatum that if Corbin did not increase its price, Scovill would re-

American Hardware Corporation, joining Corbin and Russwin in 1902, contributed to the 1914-1917 war effort by manufacturing gas mask filters, weapon components, marine hardware, and mortar fuses.

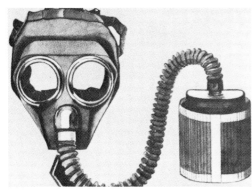

duce its price so low that Corbin would have to stop producing them.

Philip Corbin instructed the Scovill messenger to return and tell his boss that the way to hunt muskrats was to wait until they stick their heads above water, then shoot. "Now if Mr. Scovill wants to play a muskrat game he can, but every time his head shows above the water, I'll bring him down," said Corbin. Scovill subsequently met Philip and Frank Corbin at the old Humphrey House restaurant in New Britain, ending the session as friends.

Like Russell & Erwin, P&F Corbin put the manufacture of builders hardware on the back burner during World War I, producing hand grenades for the war effort. During World War II the company joined its sister firm, producing torpedo components.

CORBIN CABINET LOCK CO.

The Corbin Cabinet Lock Co. began as a separate department of P&F Corbin, manufacturing cabinet locks. Because it soon became evident that the class of locks was distinct from the normal Corbin products, a new stock company with $100,000 in capital was incorporated in 1882. The officers were the same as those of P&F Corbin. But it was George W. Corbin, elected secretary of the new firm in 1897, and Carlisle H.

Baldwin, elected president and treasurer in 1908, who were credited with being the firm's most influential early guiding forces.

The products included cabinet locks for chests, drawers, wardrobes, cupboards, and lockers, plus equipment for automobiles, cash registers, steel furniture, vending machines, pay telephones, gasoline and oil pumps, padlocks, trunk and suitcase locks, mailboxes, apartment house letter boxes, home savings banks, friction catches, hinge hasps, cardholders, straps, and brackets.

AMERICAN HARDWARE CORPORATION

Despite their rivalry in the builders' hardware market, the companies merged March 13, 1902, forming the American Hardware Corporation for the purpose of economy in administration, savings in purchases, and the elimination of duplication in manufacture. The stock in the companies was held largely by the same people, mostly New Britain residents. The combined output of the Russell & Erwin Manufacturing Co. and P&F Corbin was almost one-half the entire production of the builders' hardware industry. The same trades were involved in the production process, and it was decided a union was in the best interest of the stockholders.

Philip Corbin was named as the first president of the American Hardware Corporation for his business ability. He was still president at the time of his death on November 3, 1910.

Originally a holding company with $5 million in capital stock, American Hardware Corporation initially functioned with each division continuing to be run by its own board of directors and officers. But on September 18, 1911, the corporation formally assumed the operation of the plants, and the general manager superseded the divisions' officers.

The company's locks now provide security and decoration in places such as the Waldorf Astoria Hotel and the Rockefeller Center in New York City.

THE CORBIN MOTOR VEHICLE CORPORATION

Another subsidiary, the Corbin Motor Vehicle Corporation, was formed in 1903 for the manufacture of a four-cylinder gas-powered car called the Corbin. It quickly became known for its Yankee craftsmanship and trouble-free performance. Corbin engineers made constant improvements, including the creation of a shaft drive to replace the chain version and a water cooling system to replace the old air system. Wear and tear on parts was eliminated as much as possible through the profuse use of bearings.

The Corbin car set a speed record of 62.1 miles per hour and an economy record of 27.4 miles per gallon, but unfortunately became a casualty of what was termed the "economic quicksand of the 1907 money panic." Production ceased in 1912, eight years after the first Corbin car rolled off the assembly line. Of the 500 produced, eight are still known to be in existence.

CORBIN SCREW COMPANY

With the formation of the American Hardware Corporation, the screw departments of the Russell & Erwin Manufacturing Co. and P&F Corbin, begun in 1876, were incorporated as the Corbin Screw Co. in 1903. Its purpose was to supply the other divisions with screws used in their products.

The Corbin Screw Co. succumbed to overseas competition in 1950, when purchasing screws became more economical than manufacturing them.

EMHART CORPORATION

The biggest merger was in 1964, when the American Hardware Corporation joined the Emhart Manufacturing Co., a leading American manufacturer of glass containers with overseas investments. The Emhart name was chosen because it was recognized worldwide and allowed the American Hardware Corporation to more firmly establish itself in the international marketplace.

Because the New Britain plant was outdated, ground was broken for a new plant on November 12, 1966, on 133 acres on Episcopal Road in Berlin. The 800,000-square-foot manufacturing facility that was built there consists of two major single-story buildings connected by a two-story office building. The move to the new plant began March 6, 1969, and was completed the following September without one day of work being missed.

There are now more than 1,000 employees at the Episcopal Road plant, led by Fred Hollfelder, president of the Commercial Hardware Division.

Emhart Industries, with headquarters in Farmington, Connecti-

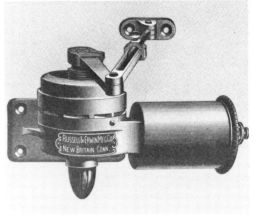

The Columbia pneumatic door check, introduced by Russell & Erwin in the late 1890s, could be mounted reversibly for either right- or left-hand doors.

cut, continued to grow through the 1980s. In 1987 a restructuring of the corporation grouped the product lines into three product areas: Industrial Products, including Russwin, Corbin, and Kwikset; Consumer Products, a group that included True Temper and Bostik; and Electronic Systems.

In 1989 Emhart Corporation was acquired by the Black and Decker Corporation of Towson, Maryland. Corbin and Russwin Hardware were incorporated into the Power Tools and Home Improvement Group of Black and Decker.

Modern architectural hardware, such as mortise locks, unit locks, and security bolts, are being produced today for use on commercial, institutional, educational, and health care buildings.

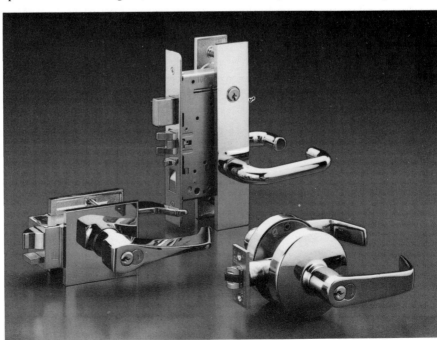

CONNECTICUT NATURAL GAS CORPORATION

Gas, the invisible substance that heats our homes, cooks our meals, and heats our water, has been serving New Britain residents since 1857. Back then, however, gas had another service to perform—lighting homes. In 1857 the New Britain Gas Light Company, created two years earlier by authority of the Connecticut General Assembly, began operating. The New Britain Gas Light Company is still in existence but is now known as Connecticut Natural Gas Corporation (CNG), a company created in 1968 through the merger of the New Britain Gas Light Company and the Hartford Gas Company.

The members of the first board of directors of the New Britain Gas Light Company used $30,000 in capital to start the company. They were the same men who established many of New Britain's other industries. They included men such as Henry E. Russell, Sr., a founder of the Russell & Erwin Manufacturing Co.; G.M. Landers, a founder of Landers, Frary & Clark; and Frederick T. Stanley, founder of The Stanley Works, who later became New Britain's first mayor.

The gaslights of the day were

the obvious origin of the company's name, but as time and technology progressed the original purpose of the firm was replaced by the need for gas for cooking and heating.

The population of New Britain when the company was founded was roughly 4,000, and business was limited. Of the 4,000 residents, only 84 were customers of the New Britain Gas Light Company. This light usage was largely due to the price the company set for its product: four dollars per 1,000 cubic feet made gas a luxury for most New Britain residents. The only forms of illumination most could afford were candles, lanterns, and oil lamps.

The company's business increased dramatically during the latter years of the Civil War; it was supplying almost all of its gas to the factories, which were operating day and night. The factories were supplying the Union Army with the materials it needed to wage a successful war.

Although in the short run the Civil War increased the business of the New Britain Gas Light Company, it caused problems for the organization in the long run. The concentration of service to industry was at least in part responsible for the company's failure to extend its gas mains in anticipation of increased residential business in the future.

Former New Britain Mayor Edward Scott celebrates the 100th anniversary of the New Britain Gas Light Company on May 26, 1955, with the wives of the company's officers and two unidentified customers of the company on the left. From Mayor Scott to the right are Mrs. H.J. Sloper, Estelle Rice, Mrs. E.G. Rhodes, Mrs. W.H. Judd, Carlotta Sloper, and Mrs. A.H. Scott.

Nevertheless, by 1870 business had increased enough for the company to abandon The Works, its original gas plant, located on what was then Commercial Street. A new plant was built at what was then the corner of Pine and Meadow streets, in the process gaining better access to the Berlin Branch Railroad.

At the end of the Civil War in 1865, the price of gas had risen to six dollars per 1,000 cubic feet, plus two dollars per year for all customers who did not use a minimum of $12 annually. In comparison with today's prices, the cost is now roughly one-third less. With the increased business in 1870, however, the price of gas was reduced to five dollars per 1,000 cubic feet, and more gas mains were installed in central streets to meet the growing demand.

That growth continued for more than 20 years with more residents of New Britain opting to light their homes with gas, while the city also lighted its streets with gas.

Things began to change in 1899, however, when the New Britain Gas Light Company lost its contract for lighting the city streets. Electric lights were installed instead. The company also found itself competing with the electric company for the business of lighting private resi-

Displayed at the Hartford City Gas Light Company in the 1920s are several gas appliances typical of the era. The 1920s was a decade of considerable growth in the use of gas for cooking and heating purposes.

A wedding cake was cut in celebration of the 1968 merger between the Hartford Gas Company and the New Britain Gas Light Company. Connecticut Natural Gas was the result of the merger. Cutting the cake are mayors Ann Uccello of Hartford and Paul Manafort of New Britian, with Robert H. Willis (left) and Edgar G. Rhodes.

dences. More and more of the industrial plants that relied so heavily on the New Britain Gas Light Company during the Civil War were installing their own lighting systems.

Times were changing. As technology progressed businesses such as the New Britain Gas Light Company replaced candles and oil lamps as the primary means of illumination. Technology was still progressing, however, replacing gaslights with electric lights.

But the New Britain Gas Light Company changed along with the times. The potentials of gas as a heating fuel were just beginning to be recognized. The more important uses of gas and what it could mean for the growth of the gas business made the gas lighting business seem insignificant.

The company introduced gas stoves in 1898. By 1906 there were 33 miles of street mains, more than 20 miles of services, approximately 3,600 gas meters, and the same number of customers. There were also some 1,800 stoves in operation in New Britain, plus hundreds of hot plates that had been sold since 1899.

With the gaslight business fading fast, the New Britain Gas Light Company plunged into the heating

and cooking aspects of the business with vigor.

The firm continued to prosper and grow. Its service area increased to include Berlin and Newington. The miles of gas mains the company laid in city streets almost tripled within the first 20 years of the century. By 1925 there had been 16,000 gas meters installed. More than 12,000 gas ranges were in use. There were also thousands of hot plates, water heaters, and room heaters. By 1949 the company was using 124 miles of pipe to serve 20,000 customers.

For most of its existence the New Britain Gas Light Company used manufactured gas to supply its customers. But, in 1952, it converted to natural gas, pumped from its source in Texas and Louisiana. It came via the Tennessee Gas Pipeline Co., then the longest natural gas pipeline in the world. The connection with the pipeline was made at the top of Bunnell Street, one of the side streets off the west side of Wooster Street. It was also at the Bunnell Street plant that special chemicals were added to give the gas the smell of rotten eggs, the telltale sign of a gas leak.

Because every gas burner on every piece of gas-burning equipment on the system had to be adjusted when the company switched from manufactured to natural gas, 200 specially trained men were assigned to handle the conversion. Although expensive, the changeover was made without any extra charge to the company's customers.

Anticipated annual savings of approximately $232,000 the first year prompted simultaneous meetings of the stockholders of the Hartford Gas Company and the New Britain Gas Light Company, conducted August 22, 1968, to consider a merger. The stockholders overwhelmingly ap-

proved the plan. In Hartford, 83.8 percent of the 500,000 common shares were voted in favor of the merger, while in New Britain, 84 percent of the 92,291 common shares voted favorably.

The merger was approved by the State Public Utility Commission four days later, while the Internal Revenue Service's okay was received August 30. The merger became reality on September 1, 1968, creating Connecticut Natural Gas Corporation.

Headquartered at 100 Columbus Boulevard in Hartford, CNG now has 675 employees serving 137,000 gas customers in 22 communities of the greater Hartford/New Britain area and Greenwich.

The present strength and importance of Connecticut Natural Gas Corporation has been accomplished by pioneering in areas unimagined in 1857. Space heating, air conditioning, and a variety of industrial and commercial innovations using gas are examples of the way in which the utility has improved and progressed over the years. Today pioneering in new technology continues in order to provide the most efficient service possible for the customers of Connecticut Natural Gas.

Connecticut Natural Gas Corporation's Operating and Administrative Center is located at 100 Columbus Boulevard in Hartford.

THE NEW BRITAIN MEMORIAL HOSPITAL

This is the story of a hospital that has responded to the special needs of the disabled throughout the course of its history. The New Britain Memorial Hospital, built during the administration of George J. Coyle, mayor of New Britain, was specially chartered as a 45-bed municipal hospital by the State of Connecticut in 1941. Then, as now, the hospital made a commitment to provide quality care to individuals with physical disabilities.

For a quarter-century Joseph C. Andrews, president of the hospital, led Memorial through an era of growth and development. He had gained an intimate knowledge of its facilities, operation, and personnel. The goal was to provide a home-like atmosphere for those residing at the hospital. Social-recreational activities were provided in addition to medical and rehabilitation services. A hospital classroom also enabled children from both the hospital and the community to pursue their educa-

Education and training help to ensure the successful return of the patient to home and family.

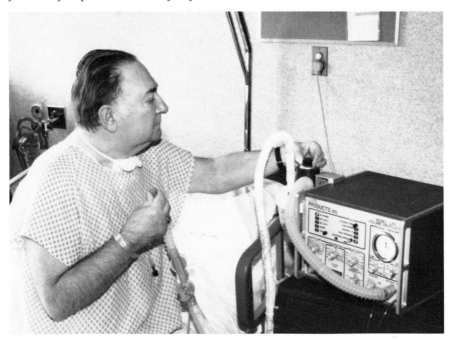

tion. Dr. Katherine C. Ill, the current president and chief executive officer, comments, "It was not to be a quiet rest home."

In response to the increasing demands for professional medical services, the hospital expanded to 72 beds in 1948. Another significant

Every hospital employee assumes a vital role in the total care of New Britain Memorial's patients.

step in growth was taken in 1960 with the opening of a two-story building, bringing the bed capacity up to 195.

As concepts of rehabilitation changed, the hospital began to take a more aggressive approach toward the treatment and rehabilitation of patients. Ideas of independent community living for the disabled were seriously considered. Many of the founders of New Horizons, an organization that promotes independent living for the physically challenged, were residents of New Britain Memorial. Since 1986, 35 residents have been discharged from the hospital to New Horizons Village in Unionville.

Today the goal remains to provide quality rehabilitation and medical services to the physically and medically disabled. An interdisciplinary team of health care professionals assists patients in their endeav-

Striving toward independence in activities of daily living is a major goal for rehabilitative patients.

aged to take an active role in the patient's total plan of care. A team of professionals teaches family members how to best assist their loved one carry over skills learned in therapy. Together the patient and family learn strategies that promote independent living and reinvolvement in community life.

The hospital provides extensive physician coverage, comprehensive individualized rehabilitation services, 24-hour nursing care, and other medical support services. Memorial concentrates on providing four rehabilitation programs: Stroke, Traumatic Brain Injury, Pulmonary Rehabilitation, and General Rehabilitation Services. The hospital continues to care for individuals with chronic lung disease, developmental disabilities, and other chronic diseases.

In keeping with the concept of encouraging independence and the return to community living, the hospital opened an outpatient clinic during the summer of 1989. The clinic enables a patient to live at home yet receive needed medical and rehabilitative treatment in a hospital setting.

As a teaching hospital New Britain Memorial is affiliated with the University of Connecticut School of Medicine, New York University, Boston University, and Pennsylvania State University, among others. Decades of experience, diversity of service, and the complexity of medical and rehabilitative issues make this licensed 200-bed hospital a unique and rewarding place to learn.

Continuing renovations to the physical plant and further development of professional services and programs earmark The New Britain Memorial Hospital's current agenda. Dr. Ill confirms, "The hospital continues its commitment to excellence in care of patients with disabilities and education of care-givers."

ors to reach a higher degree of independence and community integration. Although some individuals are hospitalized for extended periods of time, Memorial has an impressive record in assisting patients who receive rehabilitation services return to their homes and families.

The average length of stay for individuals who have suffered a stroke is five to six weeks, with 75 percent discharged to home. Seventy-seven percent of the patients receiving pulmonary rehabilitation services also return to home. Some stay at the

hospital for two to three weeks; others are discharged to home with a ventilator within five to six weeks. Patients with traumatic brain injury have the longest hospital rehabilitation stay, with an average of 21 weeks. Seventy-five percent of all those involved in this program are able to return home.

Families of patients are encour-

SOUTHERN NEW ENGLAND TELEPHONE

The first telephone exchange in Connecticut was in New Haven. It began January 28, 1878, two years after Alexander Graham Bell invented the device that revolutionized the world. There were 21 customers in the New Haven exchange, but it was not long before others in Connecticut saw the value of telephones and became subscribers of the company that soon became Southern New England Telephone (SNET).

Interest in telephones grew rapidly. By the early 1900s there were 850 telephone subscribers in New Britain, a time when its population was 28,202 and it was referred to as an "early-to-bed town."

New Britain has grown a lot since then; so has SNET. The New Britain office, formally called the Central Resident Service Center (CRSC), now handles 172,000 customers in 12 towns—New Britain, Berlin, Plainville, Newington, Southington, Meriden, Middletown, East Hampton, Moodus, Bristol, Haddam, and Wallingford. In those towns there are

From its offices at 102 West Main Street, Southern New England Telephone's New Britain exchange serves subscribers with personalized service reminiscent of the area's early "hello girl" operators.

45 telephone exchanges, or the same prefix of three numbers. The New Britain exchanges, for instance, are 223, 224, 225, 229, 826, and 827.

The first SNET office in New Britain was in the old Railroad Arcade Building, but is now located in a two-story "stilts" building on West Main Street between the Federal Savings Bank and the old post office. The company moved to the redevelopment building with parking underneath it in 1969. Another multistoried structure located on Court Street, almost directly behind the West Main Street office, houses telephone switching machinery.

The early telephone operators were called "hello girls," arriving at work on bicycles. Every time a customer picked up a telephone, he or she spoke to an operator. The operator would politely ask, "Number, please?" Instead of calling the seven-digit numbers used today, the customer would give the operator a two-digit number. It was not until September 21, 1946, that the direct-dial system was introduced to New Britain.

Extended local calling service, often referred to as "toll-free calling," went into operation in June 1987. It allows New Britain ex-

New operations began for directory assistance at Southern New England Telephone's New Britain exchange in September 1974.

change subscribers to call the Hartford exchange, and vice versa, without paying a long-distance fee.

Although there are no more telephone operators working at the New Britain office, SNET does employ approximately 150 people there. They include business office personnel, customer service representatives, installers, and central office technicians. All employees go through training courses. The customer service representatives, for instance, are trained for 12 weeks, learning things such as how to handle disgruntled subscribers, how to order new telephones, how to order a transfer of phone service from one residence to another, and how to order repairs. They issue from 10,000 to 13,000 orders per month.

The state's emergency service dispatchers are trained to operate the new enhanced 911 system on the second floor of the West Main Street building. Customers can pay their bills at the West Main Street office. They can also order any type of telephone, from Telecommunications Devices for the Deaf (TDD) to a traditional wall phone.

It is a far cry from being asked, "Number, please?"

NEW BRITAIN GENERAL HOSPITAL

Founded in 1893, New Britain General Hospital first opened its doors five years later to treat Spanish-American War veterans. It opened permanently to serve the community on May 1, 1899. Since then it has grown to become the seventh-largest hospital in Connecticut.

Today it is a 432-bed major teaching hospital affiliated with The University of Connecticut School of Medicine and several other educational institutions. It is a primary referral center for central Connecticut, serving a population of 250,000 and offering a comprehensive range of sophisticated diagnostic, therapeutic, and rehabilitative services.

New Britain General's commitment to providing central Connecticut with the finest health care available is exemplified by its excellent medical staff of more than 200 attending physicians and an additional 200 associated practitioners.

New Britain General Hospital has developed into a major medical center serving the central Connecticut area.

They are supported by more than 2,000 professional, technical, and ancillary personnel.

Originally located in the Smith House on Grand Street, the hospital now consists of nine interconnected buildings and several other structures, providing more than 500,000 square feet of floor space on a 15-acre campus.

The most recent addition, a 50,000-square-foot ambulatory care building, was opened in 1986. It houses the second-largest ambulatory, or same-day, surgery center in the state, as well as complete outpatient clinics, pre-admission testing areas, and a modern admitting department.

That same year the city constructed a 500-car parking garage on hospital land. It is conveniently located adjacent to the Ambulatory Care Building and the hospital's main entrance.

As time passed, New Britain

Originally built as the residence of J.B. Smith in 1880, this building became New Britian's hospital in 1898, just in time for Spanish-American War veterans. The location was on Grand Street, opposite Walnut Hill Park.

General not only established a reputation for excellence but also placed itself on the cutting edge of medical technology.

A helipad sits atop the parking garage with direct access to the hospital's trauma and coronary emergency facilities. The latest in diagnostic imaging technology is available, including Magnetic Resonance Imaging (MRI) and the advanced CT 9800 Computed Tomography whole body scanner.

New Britain General has not only kept pace with advances in both medicine and technology, but it has also established centers of excellence in areas such as cardiology, neurosurgery, neonatology, perinatology, radiology, maternity services, emergency care, and eye services. In fact, the New Britain General ophthalmology section enjoys a world-renowned reputation.

"Since the first Spanish-American War veteran walked through the doors of the Smith House, New Britain General has been committed to excellence," says president Laurence A. Tanner. "Here, caring and quality are a way of life."

KAESTLE BOOS ASSOCIATES, INC.

Awards and recognition for specialized design of municipal, educational, and commercial buildings are the trademark of Kaestle Boos Associates, Inc. The firm has been located in New Britain for more than 25 years and has designed several landmark buildings in New Britain.

When John Kaestle began his architectural firm in 1963, he had no staff and used an old door for a drafting table. Presently the firm consists of more than 40 professionals and uses a state-of-the-art computerized design and drafting (CADD) system.

Since founding the firm, Kaestle was joined in partnership by Charles W. Boos and the firm officially became Kaestle Boos Associates, Inc., in 1968. Theodore J. Stoutenberg, Alan I. Daninhirsch, and David W. King became partners in the early 1980s, each having started with the firm as a staff architect. Kaestle Boos Associates, Inc., emphasized then, as now, that a principal would always work directly with the client—a philosophy of "principal involvement" that has been directly associated with the success of the business.

The firm's first office was on the top floor of the old Booth Block, formerly at the corner of Main and Church streets. However, in November 1966 the firm was preparing to move, since the building was slated to be demolished. Kaestle was downtown to watch a parade with his children, noticed a fire in the building, and raced upstairs, rescuing all the architectural drawings. The firm was able to continue operations there until it moved the following month.

Continuous growth

throughout the years made it necessary for the firm to frequently seek additional office space. From the Booth Block, the firm relocated to One Prospect Street and later to 30 Bank Street, both of which were designed by Kaestle Boos Associates, Inc. Then, in 1981, the partners restored the D.B. Capron House on High Street, erecting a major addition to accommodate more growth. The 8,000- square-foot Italianate Victorian was the headquarters of the firm for several more years. The continuing success of Kaestle Boos Associates, Inc., has since required a recent relocation to a spacious 20,000-square-foot building designed by the firm on Slater Road.

There are numerous examples of contributions to New Britain that Kaestle Boos Associates, Inc., has made over the years. In 1966 the firm was selected to design the New Britain Police headquarters and received the Connecticut Building Congress Award for the design.

Since that first major commission, the firm designed many other significant New Britain buildings. Outstanding examples in the city include three major facilities at Cen-

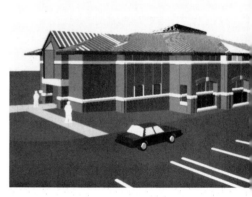

Kaestle Boos Associates, Inc.'s headquarters was located in this restored Italianate Victorian House on High Street (below) from 1981 to 1989, when the expanding firm moved into a new, larger facility of its own design on Slater Road, shown here in a computer-generated rendering (above).

tral Connecticut State University, the Copernicus Science and Industrial Arts Center, the Elihu Burritt Library, and Memorial Hall; the Superior Court building; the post office on Chestnut Street; and the Liberty Square office complex.

Acknowledged by clients and peers through an AIA Honor Award for the design of the American Red Cross building in Farmington, as well as the Certificate of Excellence in Architecture for the conversion of a former school into the Cromwell Municipal Center, Kaestle Boos Associates, Inc., has established a reputation for excellence in design and professional services. The firm continues to expand to provide superior architectural services to an increasing list of clients, while maintaining the same philosophy of involvement upon which the firm was founded.

THE HERALD

Since its founding in 1880 *The Herald* has been the chronicler of events big and small in the lives of New Britain residents. It has recorded births, school achievements, marriages, election results, and deaths, in addition to front-page stories on fires, blizzards, and hurricanes. It combines community news with stories from Associated Press and United Press International wires.

Begun as a weekly published by the Adkins Brothers Printing Co., the four-page newspaper became a daily in 1883. It was then owned by Charles E. Woodruff of Berlin. In 1887 the newspaper was bought by Frank Blanchard of New York. Robert J. Vance was named editor, and his weekly, *The Observer*, consolidated with *The New Britain Herald*. A member of the Vance family has been at the helm of *The Herald* ever since. Three of the publishers have been women.

Upon the death of Robert J. Vance in 1902, his widow, Matilda O'Connor Vance, took over until her elder son, Johnstone Vance, returned from Navy service in World War I to become editor and publisher. Upon his death, his brother, Robert C. Vance, served until his death in 1959, when their sister, Agnes Vance Weld, assumed the titles and held them until 1975. The present editor and publisher is Judith Vance Weld Brown, daughter of Agnes Vance and Gardner C. Weld, who acted as co-publisher.

Although extras have not been printed since 1951, candidates for elective office and their supporters still go to *The Herald* newsroom on election night while staff members post results. Gone, however, are the days when readers used to gather outside the old Church Street office window to read the hand-set news on a bulletin board, or to watch a world series game on the "Playograph," where the sports staff recorded each play on a metal baseball diamond display board.

In the modern new building on Herald Square, off Chestnut Street, to which the company moved in

The old Herald building as it looked in 1892, when townspeople gathered there to read the latest news hand-set on a bulletin board.

1952, video terminals and computers have replaced the old clicking typewriters and linotype machines. The present offset press began printing the approximately 40,000 papers in 1971—the newspaper having gone through six generations of presses. The papers are circulated daily in New Britain, Berlin, Plainville, Southington, Newington, and Farmington, with the first edition, added in 1976, going to Wethersfield, West Hartford, Rocky Hill, Newington, and Farmington.

Expansion of the circulation and business departments occurred in 1986, when the company purchased a brick Victorian building on Franklin Square. The carrier force now numbers more than 1,100, with motor routes and bright-blue tubes added as the circulation goes into more areas.

In a souvenir edition commemorating *The Herald's* century mark in 1980, editor and publisher Judith W. Brown noted: "In its relationship to New Britain, *The Herald* has played a unique and special part, one that is duplicated by nothing else."

The Herald's *editorial board peruses the day's editorial page at its daily meeting in Mrs. Brown's office. From left are Henry M. Keezing, William Millerick, Judith W. Brown, Lindsley Wellman, and Eric Riess.*

THE HOLIDAY INN OF NEW BRITAIN

While Holiday Inns can be found throughout the United States, the one in New Britain has a unique aspect to its history: It is the only Howard Johnson's Restaurant and Motor Lodge that has ever been converted into a Holiday Inn.

Built by Hartford developer David Chase in 1972 as a 120-room Howard Johnson's Restaurant and Motor Lodge at 65 Columbus Boulevard, New Britain, it was sold in 1978 to the Konover Hotel Corp. of East Hartford and Donald Wallace of New Britain. Then, in 1979, following a brief period when the six-story hotel was closed to allow for extensive renovations, it was reopened as a Holiday Inn.

The centerpiece of the new Holiday Inn was—and remains—Humphrey's, the hotel's restaurant and lounge. It takes its name from Humphrey House, "the first structure in the center of New Britain for the accommodation of travelers." The original Humphrey House was

founded in 1843, when John W. Humphrey of nearby Wethersfield opened a hotel in an old building on Main Street, east of Central Park. That building was replaced in 1850 by a new structure of brick with a stone foundation, three stories plus an attic and a basement. According to a description in a Holiday Inn menu, the original Humphrey House "became a comfortable home for the traveling public and a residence for some local people. Its sleeping rooms were large and clean, its table well furnished. And its large hall on the third floor served for social functions such as balls, concerts, lectures, exhibitions, and political rallies."

In 1987, 45,000 people were guests at the Holiday Inn of New Britain. At the same time, 92,000 meals were served in the Holiday Inn's restaurant, lounge, and banquet facilities. The hotel's 120 sleeping rooms comprise 56 King Leisure rooms, 12 special rooms, and 52 standard rooms. The King Leisure rooms include one king-size bed and a work area designed especially for corporate travelers. The special rooms are

Some guests stop to smell the flowers during a relaxing visit at the Holiday Inn of New Britain.

the economy rooms and include a single double bed. The standard rooms include two double beds.

The Holiday Inn also boasts a 12- by 36-foot heated indoor swimming pool. It also has a sunbathing balcony enclosed by a concrete wall to ensure the guests' privacy.

The transformation from a Howard Johnson's to a Holiday Inn also included a change in the type of restaurant located in the hotel. It went from a 24-hour counter-service restaurant when it was Howard Johnson's to a family-service dining room when it became Humphrey's.

More renovations were undertaken in 1982 and again in 1986, when the lounge, restaurant, sleeping rooms, and lobby were all done over. In early 1988 the Konover Hotel Corp. spent approximately $400,000 on new carpeting in the sleeping rooms and to change the decor in the corridors.

The majority of the hotel's guests are from the business community. Many are salesmen visiting area companies or the out-of-town employees of international companies that are in New Britain for meetings at their firms' world headquarters. The Holiday Inn of New Britain has also become a "transient

Business and leisure travelers relax with cocktails in the lobby of New Britain's Holiday Inn.

The Holiday Inn features spacious, well-appointed rooms, perfect for families.

stop" for tourists passing through the area on their way into New England.

But the hotel also caters to companies such as Dunn & Bradstreet, which has conducted training seminars on time management and other topics there. It has twice been used for state conventions of the Loyal Order of Moose. Since the home stadium of the New Britain Red Sox, a Double AA professional baseball team, is nearby, the Holiday Inn hosts all the teams that play the Boston Red Sox minor-league club. It also frequently hosts the teams that challenge Central Connecticut State University's (CCSU) athletic teams.

In addition to a 425-seat ballroom, there are four smaller meeting rooms, each large enough to seat 40 people. There is the Gaslight Room, which includes a bar; it was originally used by the former Howard Johnson's as its lounge. There are also the Stanley Room, the Belvidere Room, and the Connecticut Room. Roughly 50 wedding receptions are held every year at the Holiday Inn.

National history was also made at the Holiday Inn of New Britain on July 8, 1987. That is when the hotel was used as a command center for the White House Press Corps cov-

ering a visit by President Ronald Reagan. The ballroom was outfitted with hundreds of telephones so reporters from around the world could call their stories into their individual news organizations.

But there is some other history connected with the Holiday Inn. For one thing, it is located on the site of the old Stanley Arena. Hundreds of sporting events were held in the arena, including at least

one of former heavyweight boxing champion Floyd Patterson's early bouts as a middleweight. It is also the home of the New Britain Club, a social club where prominent local men and women can sit and talk, read, or just meditate. Located since the early 1920s in the former Burritt Hotel on West Main Street, the New Britain Club moved to the Holiday Inn in 1979. Although it was exclusively for male members for most of its existence, the club began accepting women in the early 1980s. Its first female president, Lois Bloomstran, was elected in 1988. The club has one room in the Holiday Inn decorated with fine paintings and leather upholstered chairs.

Donald Wallace bought out Konover's share of the business on September 1, 1988, becoming the sole owner of the Holiday Inn of New Britain. His daughter, Jill Denver, became the general manager. They are pledged to uphold the traditions established with the Humphrey.

New Britain's Holiday Inn serves the needs of the business community with suites that are ideal for meetings or receptions of six to eight people.

This 1872 photo shows the employees of Stanley Tool out-
side the plant at Church and Elm Streets. Courtesy, Local
History Room of the New Britain Public Library

PATRONS

The following individuals, companies, and organizations have made a valuable commitment to the quality of this publication. Windsor Publications and Family Service, Inc., gratefully acknowledge their participation in *New Britain: The City of Invention.*

Connecticut Natural Gas Corporation*
Emhart Corporation Hardware Division*
First Church of Christ, Congregational*
A.H. Harris & Sons, Inc.*
The *Herald*
Heritage Party Sales, Inc.
The Holiday Inn of New Britain*
Kaestle Boos Associates, Inc.*

New Britain General Hospital*
The New Britain Memorial Hospital*
Peter Paul Electronics Co., Inc.*
Precision Screw Products, Inc.*
Quinn Associates, Inc.*
Schaller Oldsmobile, Inc.*
Southern New England Telephone*
Spring Brook Ice & Fuel Service*
Town and Country Yellow Cab Co., Inc.*

*Partners in Progress of *New Britain: The City of Invention.* The histories of these companies and organizations appear in Chapter 7, beginning on page 95.

BIBLIOGRAPHY

In researching this book, extensive use was made of the files at the New Britain Public Library Local History Room, the archives of the Connecticut State Library, and The Herald. Newspapers used included the *Herald*, the *Hartford Courant*, the *Hartford Times*, the *New Britain Record*, the *Journal and Chronicle*, the *New Britain News, North and South*, and the *True Citizen*. City records contained in Berlin and New Britain town and city clerk offices and elsewhere were also used, along with the scrap books of former Mayors George A. Quigley and John L. Sullivan, which are at the New Britain Public Library. Company catalogues, institutional and corporate histories, numerous government reports, cemetery records, family histories, and other similar materials were used in preparing this book. Notes, which include a detailed listing of newspaper article dates, along with copies of some documents, will be given to the New Britain Public Library. What follows is a select bibliography of sources.

Adams, Edith A. *The High School, New Britain, Connecticut 1850-1950*. Published by city of New Britain, 1950.

Andrews, Alfred. *Genealogy and Ecclesiastical History of New Britain*. Chicago: A.H. Andrews, 1867.

Bickford, Christopher P. *Farmington in Connecticut*. Canaan, New Hampshire: Phoenix Publishing in association with the Farmington Historical Society, 1982.

Blejwas, Stanislaus A. "A Polish Community in Transition: The Origins and Evolution of Holy Cross Parish, New Britain, Connecticut." *Polish American Studies*, 1977, no. 1 and 1978, nos. 1-2.

Brooks, Kate. *A History of The South Congregational Church*. New Britain: 1938.

Buczek, Daniel S. *Immigrant Pastor*. Waterbury: Heminway Corporation, 1974.

Burpee, Charles W. *History of Hartford County Connecticut*. Hartford: The S.J. Clarke Publishing Co., 1928.

Burritt, Elihu. *Colonial History of the Farmington Family of Towns*. Manuscript, n.d.

Camp, David N. *History of New Britain*. New Britain: William B. Thompson and Company, 1889.

—————. *Recollections of a Long and Active Life*. Concord, New Hampshire: The Rumford Press, 1917.

—————. *A Half Century of the South Congregational Church*. New Britain: the South Congregational Church, 1893.

Churchill, Frederick H. Memorial book prepared by his wife for their children. N.p., 1881.

Connecticut. Bureau of Labor Statistics. *The Case, Lockwood and Brainard Co*. Hartford: 1885-1916.

—————. General Assembly. *Records of the Joint Standing Committee on Towns and Probate Districts, 1850*. Hartford: State Library Archives, 1850.

—————. Highway Department. "Hartford Area Traffic Study." Vol. 1., 1961.

Comstock, J.B. *History of The House of P. & F. Corbin*. New Britain: 1904.

Cooper, Stanley M. *Fifty Years of Fafnir*. New Britain: 1968.

Curti, Merle. *The Learned Blacksmith*. New York: Wilson-Erickson, Inc., 1937.

Dahl, Edward C. Paper of John Smalley D.D. for the New Britain Saturday Night Club. N.p., 1960.

Daniels, Bruce C. *The Connecticut Town*. Middletown, Connecticut: Wesleyan University Press, 1979.

Daughters of The American Revolution, Emma Hart Willard Chapter, Berlin, and Esther Stanley Chapter, New Britain. Papers on Berlin and New Britain history published in the *New Britain Herald*, 1935-1936.

Devoe, Shirley Spaulding. *The Tinsmiths of Connecticut*. Middletown, Connecticut: Wesleyan University Press in association with the Connecticut Historical Society, 1968.

Domizio, Albert F. *New Britain and The Civil War*. New Britain: 1977.

Emergency Relief Commission. *Report of the City Social Survey, New Britain, Connecticut*. Hartford: 1935.

Fellows, Dexter W., and Andrews A. Freeman. *This Way to the Big Show: The Life of Dexter Fellows*. New York: The Viking Press, 1936.

First Church of Christ, Congregational, New Britain, Connecticut. Church Records from 1754 to 1850. Library of Central Connecticut State University, New Britain.

—————. *One Hundred and Fiftieth Anniversary*. New Britain: First Church of Christ, Congregational, 1908.

First Baptist Church, New Britain: A Brief History. New Britain: 1877.

Fowler, Herbert E. *A Century of Teacher Education in*

Connecticut. New Britain: Teachers College of Connecticut, 1949.

——————. *A History of New Britain*. New Britain: New Britain Historical Society, Inc., 1960.

Gay, Julius. *Farmington Papers*. N.p., 1929.

Gentile, Louis A. "Voting Behavior, City of New Britain, 1928-1940." Paper prepared for master's course, Central Connecticut State University, New Britain Connecticut, 1976.

Greene, Thayer Ainsworth. "Elihu Burritt and the Anti-slavery Movement." Undergraduate paper, Amherst College, 1950.

Hagert, Blanche. "Jewelry Manufacturing." Master's Thesis, Trinity College, Hartford, Connecticut, 1936.

Hennessy, Thomas F. *Early Locks and Lockmakers of America*. Des Plaines, Illinois: Nickerson and Collins Publishing Co., 1976.

Kensington Congregational Church, Two Hundredth Anniversary Program. Kensington Congregational Church, 1912.

Kinnard William N., Jr. Report on the New Britain Economy for the New Britain City Plan Commission, 1957.

Larson, Kenneth A. *A Walk Around Walnut Hill, New Britain*. Brooklyn, New York, and New Britain: Kalarson, 1975.

M.E.H. Rotival & Associates. "New Britain, Hardware City of The World, Master Plans its Future." Report prepared for the City of New Britain, 1961.

Moore, E. Allen. *Four Decades with The Stanley Works, 1889-1929*. New Britain: 1950.

Moses, Robert. "Expressway Through New Britain." Report prepared for the City of New Britain, 1951.

Moret, Marta. *A Brief History of the Connecticut Labor Movement*. Storrs, Connecticut: Labor Education Center, University of Connecticut, 1982.

New Britain Centennial, 1871-1971. New Britain: 1971.

North, Catharine M. *History of Berlin, Connecticut*. New Haven: Tuttle, Morehouse and Taylor, 1916.

Northend, Charles. *Elihu Burritt: A Memorial Volume*. New York: D. Appleton & Co., 1879.

Ostapchuk, William J. "A Survey of The Development of the Hardware Industry in New Britain, 1820-1860." Master's thesis, Central Connecticut State College, New Britain, Connecticut, 1969.

Peck, Charles. Paper on the early history of New Britain for the Saturday Night Club. New Britain: 1888.

Porter, Maxwell S. *The Parks of New Britain* (Annual Report of the park commissioners). New Britain: 1901.

Porter, Noah. "A historical discourse delivered at the celebration of the 100th anniversary of the erection of the Congregational Church in Farmington, Connecticut, 1872." 1873. Reprinted 1972.

Ratner, Lorman. *Powder Keg: Northern Opposition to the Antislavery Movement, 1831-1840*. New York: Basic Books, Inc., 1968.

Shepard, James. *New Britain Patents and Patentees*. New Britain: 1901.

——————. *History of Saint Mark's Church, New Britain, Connecticut*. New Britain: 1907.

Sloper, W.T. *The Life and Times of Andrew Jackson Sloper*. New Britain: 1949.

Smalley, John, D.D. *Sermons on various subjects*. Middletown, Connecticut: Hart and Lincoln, 1814.

Stanley, Frederick T. "Historical Reminiscences of New Britain." Unpublished paper, New Britain, 1874.

Strother, Horatio T. *The Underground Railroad in Connecticut*. Middletown, Connecticut: Wesleyan University Press, 1962.

Tata, Robert Joseph. "Problems of Industrial Old Age. New Britain, Connecticut: A Case Study." Master's thesis, Syracuse University, 1961.

Tolis, Peter. *Elihu Burritt: Crusader for Brotherhood*. Hamden, Connecticut: Archon Books, 1968.

Tryon, Lillian Hart. *The Story of New Britain*. New Britain: The Esther Stanley Chapter of the Daughters of the American Revolution, 1925.

Thomas Walbert & Associates. "Route 72 Locations Studies, New Britain, Connecticut." Report prepared for the City of New Britain, 1959.

Wallace, M. Willard. *An Historical Sketch of Berlin, Connecticut*. Berlin, Connecticut: 1985.

Weld, Ralph Foster. *Slavery in Connecticut*. New Haven: The Yale University Press in association with the Tercentenary Commission of the State of Connecticut, 1935.

Wellman, Lindsley. "Our Town." Paper prepared for the New Britain Saturday Night Club, 1979.

Wolkovich-Valkavicius, William, Rev. "Portrait of Occupations, Investments and Businesses of Lithuanian Immigrants in New Britain, Connecticut." Hudson, Massachusetts: 1979.

The three generations of the Landers family pictured here all served their city well. George Marcellus Landers I was a founder of Landers, Frary and Clark;
George M. Landers II became mayor in 1906 and Charles S. Landers carried on his father's work in L.F.&C. Courtesy, Local History Room
of the New Britain Public Library

INDEX